MAD
AS
HELL

Part One: 899 Days

David N. Anderson

This Edition Published by David N. Anderson
ISBN: 978-0-9955917-0-7

Disclaimer: This is a work of non-fiction. The events and
discussions described are to the best of the author's memory. At times
events and conversations have been compressed or grouped to aid the flow
of the narrative. Names, (most) places and some details have been
changed to protect the privacy of the people involved.

For Danny and Arthur

CONTENTS

MAD AS HELL

Part One: 899 Days

FOREWORD

Why, and for whom, have I written these books (Parts One and Two)? Let alone, published them? Well, this story is for both me and you, the reader. My intention has been not only to record events as they happened in an attempt to exorcise an unpleasant experience, but I believe that elements of the story might be of use to the reader. For, but for the grace of God, goes anybody, even you. Or your spouse. Or son. Or daughter.

A general note: Some reviewers who have read early drafts have said that the narrative is too dispassionate, suggesting that I need to describe how I felt more. In order to sympathize to the narrator, they have said, the reader has to like him. I understand and respect the argument, after all it is in good literary tradition, so where I could I have incorporated the feedback. But frankly, I have not written these books to make friends or solicit sympathy. To my mind the important thing is the reporting of events and how they impacted my everyday life. Of course, I vent my frustration and I recount elements of the ensuing madness, but once the seriousness of the situation became clear, it was necessary for me to adopt a cool, methodological approach to the pickle I had found myself in. I needed to absorb and analyse details, advice and endure the drama of police interviews and court appearances – ultimately to survive long enough to see closure. Getting emotional served no purpose. In fact, it was not in my interest. If I felt myself getting angry, frustrated or just despairing, I concentrated on breathing and taking the long view. I pushed emotional reactions aside saying to myself – that's for another day. Arguably, dispassion acted as a bulwark against the insanity of the situation and helped to keep my head functional, by which I mean: putting a defence strategy together. To engage with the frustrations and anxiety was to submit to them. I had to play the long game. (In fact, I am still playing it.)

So, for the reader, I hope these books chart the steps and describe the challenges of answering a criminal charge in a court of law. Anybody of a certain age knows that life is, to a large extent, a lottery. In this respect I accept that the events described herein constitute the rubbish hand I have been dealt. I don't 'massively' resent it, but I feel obliged to get the story 'out there'. I invite you to listen and learn. At the end of Part Two I give some tips to those caught in a similar predicament. To those readers who don't think the tips are relevant to them, I suggest you make a mental note of my words anyway; you might perhaps thank me one day.

I have also included (in Part One) descriptions of a number of short overseas breaks. Though not directly relevant to the legal narrative (one reader even suggested taking them out) they were important psychological interludes to the misery. The breaks were reminders of another life and provided moments of peace, perspective and reflection. I have therefore kept them here (in Part One) both out of a sense of indulgence and a hope that they allow the reader to take time out from the enclosed miserable business. I'll give you warnings when they occur and you can skip the chapter if need be. No offence taken.

Owing to the nature of the charge, I referred to my troubles as my 'Pickle' – a term borrowed from a work colleague who found a family member in a tussle with police. In time, the madness, craziness of my existence could not be disassociated from the Pickle and so the term became 'Crazy Pickle' – a term shortlisted for the title of the book, but it was not deemed catchy enough. I tried various other connotations for the books' titles, none were totally satisfactory or media-friendly. Finally, I plumped for a line from the movie *Network*.

During the three years of bail (and before the case was dropped by the Crown Prosecution Service) I went a bit crazy. Was the madness my own making in a perfectly reasonable world? Or was the world a type of hell? A place where sane people go mad? Or was I angry and vexed to a hellish degree? Perhaps all of the above. Which leads me on to another observation. Where does one look for respite from (or sense in) the madness? For me, it was to be found in tarmac and road repairs. Or sometimes in the sky, black cats, the cosmos or whatever one describes as other-worldly. (Part One introduces this theme.)

There are three main players in this story. Me, Thames Valley Police and a German woman (a girlfriend of a former housemate) known here as Anna T. Mannheim. The story is a possibly a life-defining event. I say 'possibly' because it isn't over yet and, depending on how things pan out, it might just be an irritating, costly, draining episode.

Part One charts the day of arrest to my standing in the court dock two and a half years later. Part Two starts with me standing in the dock in front of three Magistrates and covers my trial preparation up to the point the case was dropped – two weeks before a scheduled Crown Court trial. (Part Two actually concludes with a few weeks of re-acclimatisation to the normal world and my 'final thoughts' and advice for the reader.) The books are designed to be standalone, so the reader does not have to read both. However, reading in sequence might give a fuller picture (and would increase the royalties to me and help recover the losses incurred from my Crazy Pickle, [insert Smiley Face]).

In summary, two things: Remember, I describe events and share experiences in the context of how I dealt with them. They would be different for you. I'm not your friend and I am not trying to be. Secondly, brace yourself, parts of the story are an unpleasant, challenging read. When I first broke the news of my criminal charge to a friend, he replied, 'God. Of all the things. Why couldn't it be … murder?' I know, I replied to him, I wish. So, reader, if you want a pretty story there are other places you can go.

Names have been changed to protect the innocent and guilty.

As for me, some people describe me as a closed book. Difficult to read. Whether it is a chilled, low-key nature or a variation on 'bitchy resting face', I don't know. As far as I am concerned, I'm an open book.

But after all of this you might still be left wondering 'why?' Why write up such an episode and open oneself up to lewd insinuation and the doubt of others? Aside from the exposé of Ms Anna T. Mannheim and police methods and inefficiencies, it would surely leave a cloud hanging over the author? And you are most probably right. But there is one final element to the answer to the question 'why' and it is possibly the most important – fear. If anything were to stop me (or anybody) from publishing a similar story, it is because of fear. But here is the 'but'.

I know deep down that if I didn't complete and publish this work there would come a day – my last – when I wished I had. For on my deathbed I, like many others before me, would be laughing in the face of fear, because fear is all about repercussions. If I didn't publish the book now that last day of mine would also be a day of regret. At the moment of one's passing one cannot be fearful of the repercussions of things not done in life. A lifetime of cowering 'literally' serves no purpose. So, in anticipation of my deathbed .... I present to you, *Mad As Hell* (Parts 1 and/or 2). So read on and live the three-year story not one reader would volunteer to experience for him/herself. One final word of advice (before the final chapter): know that one day you will too laugh in the face of fear. Just make sure it is not a day of regret too.

The Author 'David N. Anderson' (not my real name)

Year One (Y1)

Y1: 1. 'Intelligence'

I had never been arrested before. It wasn't so bad. In fact if I were to recommend a team of four police officers to conduct a 'raid' on your home, there is a good chance I would recommend DC Hopkins and her three colleagues. That is not to say it wasn't a crazy day. Of my then 14,225 days (spread evenly over nearly 39 years) each one had started fairly innocuously, so I was due a crazy day. It would be the start of a journey that would end two years, eleven months and four days later. Twenty-four days short of three years. 1,080 days in total. I say 'end', it was the end in the eyes of the criminal justice system when a judge formally brought legal proceedings to a conclusion in a Crown Court.

I was awake at 7.40 a.m. and looking for a reason to roll out of bed. The arrival of four plain-clothed police officers at my bedroom door was as good a reason as any. A minute or so earlier, I had heard the doorbell ring and my mother open the front door downstairs. There was a pause before I heard her climb the stairs at some speed.

'David, there are four police officers downstairs wanting to talk to you,' she said appearing at my door somewhat breathless and confused.

On my feet and totally flummoxed, I was unable to process her words when my deliberations were overtaken by the sight of a young, blonde woman clutching a file and peering at me from behind my mother. That's odd, I thought, the woman has followed my mother up the stairs.

'David?' the woman enquired politely, 'I'm DC Lauren Hopkins. Can we speak to you downstairs for a minute?'

Moments later, and somewhat bewildered, I pottered down the stairs in a T-Shirt, trousers and bare feet encountering three other plain-clothed officers along the way. The only thing that established their status as police officers were the ID badges that were attached to their belts.

Downstairs in the sitting room I took a seat on the sofa. DC Hopkins sat on an armchair in front of me. Her three colleagues remained standing. My mother took a seat in the corner of the room.

'We need to talk to David on his own,' the detective said to my mother.

'This is my home, I'm not going anywhere,' my mother replied.

I was not fussed. I wondered whether my mother was doing it for my benefit, or for her own. I didn't see any problem and shrugged.

'I don't mind,' I mumbled.

Detective Constable Hopkins turned to me and began.

'David, we have intelligence that you have downloaded indecent images of children while you lived at Meadow Road.'

Meadow Road had been my previous rented accommodation on the other side of town. Twelve months earlier I had down-sized my life to pursue various career opportunities and creative projects. I had packed in my job, sold stuff, gave stuff away, put a bunch of stuff in storage and moved back to my parents to manage this next career (life) step.

'Says who?' I replied wholly stunned suddenly realising this was serious business.

'We are not at liberty to divulge,' replied DC Hopkins.

Her words immediately struck me as odd, but, in my stunned state, I didn't argue.

3

'We have a warrant to search the house and remove any equipment or devices which can store images,' she continued.

I nodded in acknowledgement and, with a sigh, muttered, 'Okay'.

I was struggling to keep up with developments. One hundred and eighty seconds had passed and my world had changed.

'So, we're going to go upstairs and remove your computer belongings. We will then go down to the police station and have a talk.'

Surreal. Bizarre.

In a daze I walked with the four officers back up the stairs to my room. Was this a 'police raid'? It all seemed very civilised. They were all perfectly polite, so the only course of action was to be polite and reasonable in return. I had nothing to hide, but I was wracking my brains. As an adult of the Internet generation I had seen what most women would be aghast to hear described as 'regular porn', but nothing was shouting from the depths of my memory that should make me panic.

Was this related to the use of my credit card? A case of identity theft? Was my email address on some email distribution list? Had some link or other popped up on my computer and I had clicked it out of ignorance or curiosity? I was struggling to place the source of the problem, but my instinct was throwing nothing up. Halfway up the stairs I asked the detective again what had prompted the police visit.

'We have intelligence,' she repeated.

Again, I thought her choice of words was peculiar. Police officers on TV programmes referred to 'evidence' or would say things like 'we know that ...', but 'intelligence' in a non-military setting sounded bizarre.

'What is this intelligence?' I asked.

'I'm afraid I can't tell you that, but all I can say is that it relates to Meadow Road in 2007' [two years earlier].

I pressed, but the detective declined again. I turned to my mother beside us.

'I don't know what this is about. No idea,' I said. 'I have sometimes looked at adult porn on websites. No idea what this is about. I might have had pop-ups and maybe I clicked something,' I speculated in the absence of any information, 'but it's all adult stuff.'

We entered my room. I leant over my computer and unplugged the screen from the back of the Apple computer tower. I was keen that the dismantling of my prized machine was carefully managed, but no, one of the younger officers stepped forward saying he would do it. I stood back.

'We'll have to take everything,' said Lauren.

Of all the items in my possession to take – the computer, seriously? I had packed in the job to complete the editing of two full-length low-budget movies. Shot on digital video a few years earlier I had completed one film to the point where it had been screened at various venues in Oxford and London. I was now editing it down and colour-correcting the latest (and, I hoped) final version whereupon I could continue editing the second film. Both movies were sitting on the computer and the accompanying external hard drives. I had hundreds of DVD and CD back-up files and film versions on spindles lying about the room. It was, quite simply, my life's work.

'What else is there?' DC Hopkins asked.

Pointing, I mumbled something about there being three computers in the adjacent study room: an Apple eMac, a PC Toshiba laptop and an Apple Powerbook from work.

'What will you take?' I asked.

'Everything.'

'Everything?'

She nodded.

'Is there anything else?'

'Well, I have stuff in a lock-up across the road. All stuff from my house move, but there's nothing of interest there. I can happily take you over if you want.'

I was at ease being completely open. I had no intention of shadow-boxing around her questions. Moving back into my room the two officers started to pack up my computers. One officer dismantled the equipment and passed it to the other officer who logged and bagged it. What was wholly bizarre was seeing my belongings being handled by two strangers wearing white plastic gloves in my bedroom at ten minutes to eight o'clock on a midweek morning. What is this, I thought to myself, a crime scene? Were the gloves to prevent their DNA getting on the DVD, CDs and paperwork? How did DNA come into it? It was crazy. A small bookcase loaded with spindles of DVDs and CDs (used and unused) stood next to my desk. All were being picked through, examined, their contents discussed between officers and then logged on official pads.

It was suggested that I leave them to it.

I left my bedroom and suddenly found myself in a small study room next door. On the desk sat three computers: the eMac, the Toshiba laptop belonging to my mother and the Apple laptop. The detective, as ever, was by my side.

'I need to give you these,' she said searching through her papers. 'It's a copy of the warrant to search the premises.'

I took the one-page document of densely-packed text and started to read. No sooner had I read the first three words when I realised I had not absorbed their meaning. I re-read them, but then struggled to join the meaning of the fourth word to the previous word. I started again and the same happened. I worked with documents on a daily basis and with all my effort I could not make head or tail of the first line of text. I almost surprised myself at my ineptitude.

'I don't think I can read this now,' I said, wondering if there was some important information on the document that I was overlooking and thereby disadvantaging myself.

I heard stirrings in my parents' room next door. My father was up, no doubt alerted by my mother. God knows what he was going to make of four police officers in his house searching for evidence of indecent images of children, but a job had to be done. I needed to deal with it head-on, so I advised DC Hopkins that I needed to explain to my father. She understood but as I moved to the bedroom door, I found the detective on my shoulder. Why was she following me? Surely this was a private interaction? Was she afraid that I would impart some information to my seventy-six year old father? Ask him to dispose of material lurking somewhere in the house? Opening the door I saw my father adjusting his clothes and looking bewildered. He wasn't usually up at this time. I cut to the chase and gave him the details and advised that that I might have looked at some dirty-mag type porn in the vain hope he might have done the same in the 1950s before he met my mother, but knowing deep down that it was unlikely.

'Oh, oh,' he said shaking his head as if to shake free the words that were bouncing about his head. I had no intention of hanging around and left him to it.

As my services were not required for the time being, I thought it best to wash and dress. I stepped back in to my room to retrieve a T-shirt and socks and washing gear, by which time officers had loaded CD and DVD spindles into clear plastic bags. I pointed to a black case of one hundred plus DVDs under the bed.

'That case is full of DVDs – back-ups,' I said helpfully, shaking my head in disbelief. 'It's all film stuff.'

The officer pulled storage boxes from under my bed and began to sort through its contents – just files of correspondence, film paperwork, my travel folder. I almost wanted to help them and speed up the collection of material.

Having moved back temporarily the previous year, all my clothes were in cardboard boxes and bin liners under my bed, but this didn't prevent the officers taking a step towards me and observing from where I was retrieving my clothing and presumably checking to make sure I wasn't interfering with potential evidence. I headed into the bathroom and locked the door. It wasn't yet eight o'clock, but I welcomed the peace and quiet. Immediately there was a knock on the door. I opened it to find DC Hopkins asking me to keep the door open. I nodded and pushed the door to, leaving it ajar by six inches allowing a male officer to keep an eye on me.

Having washed and changed, I was asked for the keys to my VW Golf. It needed to be searched. They hadn't asked about my car, yet they knew the make and model. This wasn't an arbitrary search, I realised. These guys had done their homework.

I headed downstairs and sat in the living room with DC Hopkins. Now alone, she advised me what was going to happen. Once the search had been completed – perhaps within an hour or so – we would drive down to the police station where I would be questioned. I asked whether a solicitor was needed.

'I couldn't advise,' she replied.

I didn't watch too many crime shows on TV, but the 'suspect' in the shows I did watch (CSI, for instance) only ever asked for a solicitor when he or she had something to hide. So, I found myself thinking: if I ask for a solicitor then that implies guilt?

I asked the detective again, but she repeated that it was not her position to advise me. However, seeing that I was struggling with the predicament, she continued (albeit hesitatingly).

'If I had been arrested then I might want a solicitor in case I said something I later regretted,' she said quietly.

Her words took me by surprise. If she, a police detective, was indirectly suggesting that a solicitor wouldn't be such a bad idea, there was no 'effing way I was going to be interviewed without one. On one level it was also a little encouraging. She was almost looking out for me having been in my company for only twenty minutes.

'Sure, okay, yes, I'd like a solicitor.'

'Do you know any?' she asked.

'No, no-one at all. How would I go about getting one?'

'We can appoint one for you.'

'How much does it cost?'

'There would be no charge.'

'Well, yes, I'd like one please,' I said, relieved. 'How long would this take?'

'Depends how long it takes to pack up here and we have to wait for the solicitor.'

'Well, you can book one now as far as I am concerned.'

Allowing for a few hours for the interview, I was hoping it would all be over by the early afternoon.

For all the hubbub, DC Lauren Hopkins was professional and seemed personable, even sympathetic. But what information had led her to this place? What did she know? What was her view? If she had apparent evidence of 'wrongdoing', then was she thinking that she was looking at a suspect in denial? Or did she genuinely have no or little evidence and was largely sympathetic with the man sitting opposite and at the harsh business end of her investigations?

A police officer began bringing down bagged items of my computer stuff – external hard drives, DVDs burned with various versions of the film, blank DVDs, my iPod, my spare mobile phone, an invoice of a past holiday (which, DC Hopkins explained, acted as evidence that I had lived at Meadow Road), and all my memory sticks backing up documents. It rammed home that I wouldn't be able to do any film work at all once this had all walked out the door. My iPod was going with nearly 4GB of music and now that my G4 computer was also going, my whole music collection would be unavailable. I had LPs tucked up in storage, but no proper means to play the records. I had gone digital years before.

I was invited to review the contents of the bags and sign away the forms detailing their seizure. I was glancing at the items listed on the papers, but once again, I was having difficulty focusing on the words and details. I recognised the odd word, 'Lacie', but signed them all anyway. I was signing away my life. Somewhere deep inside, I knew that if I protested at a later date, then the police would just wave my signature around saying everything was done with my full knowledge. Nevertheless, for the time being at least everything was polite and completed in a measured manner.

At some point I was told it might be a long day and invited to get some breakfast. I hadn't eaten much in the previous few days and had been intending to treat myself to a cooked breakfast in a local café that morning. In the circumstances I was not particularity hungry, but realised I ought to eat something. I moved to the kitchen, discreetly followed by DC Hopkins, and paced back and forth while making a couple of slices of toast and tea.

The immediate shock of their arrival having passed, my mother slipped into normal hosting mode.

'Would you like a cup of tea?' she asked DC Hopkins.

'Oh, I don't know. No,' the detective replied weakly.

'What about your friends?' my mother asked chirpily.

'Oh, er.'

The detective stepped into the hallway and called up to her colleagues – would they like a drink? Tea? Coffee?

'No,' came the firm replies. No doubt they're busy, I thought, poking through my stuff, stripping my room of my livelihood.

'Are you sure you don't want one?' my mother asked again.

'Oh, no, no, thank you. I'm fine.'

I almost thought my mother would insist, I almost felt like jumping in and insisting myself saying enough of the police raid protocol. My mother let it go and started to chat.

'If I'd known you were coming, I'd have tidied up.'

I almost looked forward to going to the police station.

Y1: 2. Arrest

My parents had mellowed and started chatting to DC Hopkins about her background. As I paced back and forth in silence and increasing irritation, I felt I ought to appreciate the easy-going chat as it lessened the seriousness of the situation in my parents' eyes and became just another rubbish day in the life of one of their five offspring. Besides, the conversation might also give to the police an indication of the accused's background. Speaking of which, my mother turned to me and asked:

'David, you didn't let others use your computer in Meadow Road, did you?'

'Of course,' I replied, vexed the conversation had turned to matters of interest to the police. It could open a can of worms – I was thinking of friends and family members; there was no way I wanted to drag others into this. The time of the alleged offence was a time before smartphones: emails, train times, calendars, maps, news, social media, the Internet all had to be checked on a full-sized computer.

'But not Ian?' my mother continued.

'Why not? I never turned anyone down.'

'Oh, you are stupid,' my mother muttered.

Ian had been a housemate and, on the whole, a reasonable person. The reference to Ian was overheard by my father as he entered the kitchen.

'Oh no, not that oddball,' he spat.

Ian wasn't quite the 'odd ball' but I didn't want a conversation in front of the police. Besides, it was most probably a coincidence. My initial thought was that one of my twelve credit cards (used to fund the film-making over the years) had somehow been compromised.

Managing to move the conversation away from housemates, my mother asked the detective, who was now comfortably seated at the kitchen table, how long the computers would be gone. The police detective wouldn't commit herself to a date for the equipment's return.

My mother turned to me, 'So how am I going to access my email?'

Being a learner-silver-surfer meant that my mother had a handful of emailing duties with sons (one in Australia), a daughter (in Shropshire) and old friends.

'I can introduce you to Internet cafés,' I mumbled, at which my mother replied she wouldn't be visiting any Internet café. I realised she was trying to show her indignation at the inconvenience of the removal of all the computers, but I was unsure whether it was helpful.

It did, however, prompt a remark from DC Hopkins – there was to be a change of plan. The police wouldn't be taking all the computers after all. The detective advised us that they would not now be seizing the eMac and Toshiba laptop (both of which the police knew I used). This was a change of tack from earlier in the morning. Was this a good sign? Was I now being taken less seriously as a potential offender? It was no secret that there had been other tenants in the Meadow Road property – it was a matter of public record. Perhaps the 'intelligence' was indeed based on a credit card; it was common knowledge that identity theft had caused problems for all sorts of people. Or perhaps the intelligence was not specific to me? After all, there had been a number of co-tenants.

The other officers brought down more bagged-and-tagged computer equipment, piling it all up in the sitting room. The large, plain transparent bags were no different to those seen in dozens of films, documentaries and news items over the years. An awful thought occurred to me. I looked out the kitchen window overlooking the drive and parking spaces in the street. There were no patrol cars, which was a relief, only a couple of small, unmarked hatchbacks (which I assumed were the police vehicles) in the parking spaces on the far side of the street. My mother's car was parked right up close to the house's front door. I turned to her.

'Is it possible to move your car so that one of their cars can be reversed up to the front door?' I asked (and implying it would allow the police to load up their vehicles discreetly).

'Fine, no problem,' my mother replied understanding exactly what I meant rising from her seat, grabbing her keys and leaving.

DC Hopkins explained that she had to sketch a layout of the house. I led her first to the door off the hallway that opened into the garage. It housed my father's car and the usual junk to be found in any garage – toolboxes, shelves of knick-knacks and more. As I opened the door my heart sank. Were the police going to pull this place apart? Isn't that what they do? Search every possible hiding place for evidence?

'Oh right, okay,' said DC Hopkins scribbling a few notes and drawing a diagram. She didn't step forward into the garage, but took a step back into the hall seemingly content. Another good sign, I thought, I hoped.

I showed her the remaining rooms downstairs then moved upstairs and showed her a guest bedroom; she just poked her head into it. Next my parents' room and then a small adjacent room used for boxed storage (some of which was mine). Lauren just scribbled and she seemed content. There was no request to look in the attic, the garden shed or in the storage unit across the road (which I had mentioned earlier in the morning). As my mother (and I) later noted, the search warrant allowed the police to search all the rooms in the house and outbuildings. The search warrant in full read:

> *Dated: 10 February For the issue of a warrant*
> *under: Sec. 4 Protection of Children Act 1978.*
>
> *To enter: [Address] ... and search any persons*
> *therein, including any outbuildings within the*
> *curtilage of the premise and any vehicles that can*
> *be positively identified as being under the control*
> *of the occupants in the premise linked with*
> *offences of Possessing and Making Indecent*
> *Photographs of Children ... and search for:*
> *Abusive images and pseudo images of children,*
> *equipment used for storing and viewing such*
> *images and any relevant materials, including*
> *electronically stored written data. .... Authority is*
> *hereby given for any constable of the Thames*
> *Valley Police (accompanied by other person or*

*persons as necessary for the purposes of the
search) to enter said premises within three
months from the date of issue of this warrant, on
one occasion only, to search for material in
respect of which the application is made and any
persons therein. Signed Deputy District Judge
(Magistrates Court) 14: 09 hrs.*

DC Hopkins and her colleagues were quite relaxed about
not searching other rooms or outbuildings. Perhaps the
'intelligence' was weak and indeterminate and they were just
following up as a matter of obligation. Whichever it was, I was
inclined to take it as a good sign.

Returning downstairs, DC Hopkins and I sat alone in the
sitting room. She continued to complete paperwork relating to
the items being removed. Her mobile rang and she answered.

'All fine, we'll be back in an hour or so,' she said.

Up until that point this police experience had been limited
to four plain-clothes officers and confined to a small, familiar
house. It hadn't occurred to me that it had a whole other
dimension – other people wanting updates, people who had
contributed to discussions about 'the case'; people who knew
my name, housing arrangements, my vehicle details. When I
reviewed the search warrant a day or so later, I noted the
Magistrate authorising the house search had signed the
document on 10 February – a full week before the police visit.
Seven days in which I had been in absolute ignorance of what
would happen.

Her call completed and alone together once again, DC
Hopkins turned to me and said she was obliged to read me my
rights and make the formal arrest. Okay, I nodded and sighed,

grateful for the warning of what was to follow. She began slowly and spoke with a clear and consistent tone:

'David Anderson, I am arresting you on the suspicion of downloading indecent images of children. You have the right to remain silent, but anything you say may be taken down and used in evidence against you...'.

I appreciated her sensitivity when carrying out the task and wondered whether this was the result of her training or part of her personality. Or was it even influenced by thoughts that the police might be barking up the wrong tree?

More equipment was brought downstairs and more forms completed. Realising that their search would soon be concluded and I might be preoccupied for much of the rest of the day I raised the issue of going to the lavatory. DC Hopkins asked one of colleagues to accompany me. Once again the lavatory door could not be closed. I advised the twenty-something Detective Constable, who himself looked uncomfortable, that I 'would not be standing up' and might be a few minutes. And so it was that I had a few more moments to myself, nevertheless it was surreal glimpsing a stranger (a police detective, no less) standing to attention and watching me through the gap in the door.

A police vehicle was reversed up to the front door to allow the seized computer equipment to be loaded up relatively discreetly. As the police officers gathered in the hall ready for departure I bounded up the stairs to retrieve a fleece, my spectacles and a Walkman radio for the long walk back home at the end of the day. Entering my bedroom I found a breathless DC Hopkins right behind me. Again, it was a reminder that I was now being watched and followed wherever I went.

Needing a bag for the items, I emptied a small, khaki canvas shoulder bag of wooden martial arts weapons onto the bed. For a moment I wondered whether she felt uneasy thinking that the 'suspect' might suddenly turn violent, but the thought was replaced by another: might she even be inclined to question me on the legality of the possession of such items? I loaded the bag with my belongings, a hat and scarf and headed back downstairs. Now ready to go, DC Hopkins turned to me for a final time before we exited the house.

'I'm not going to cuff you,' she said, looking grave.

It took a moment for me to process her words. It hadn't occurred to me that this was a 'cuff-able' situation. I processed a mental image of myself being walked to the unmarked police vehicle in handcuffs. Did they think I'd run off? Get agitated, even violent, in the car? Probably all procedural, but still .....
Right, okay, I thought. Maybe I nodded a 'thank you', but it was another surreal moment amongst many that were coming thick and fast.

Leaving the house at shortly after 9.00 a.m. it was an uneventful half dozen steps to the car.

I turned to see a fraught mother standing in the doorway.

'Don't worry, I'm fine,' I said.

It was a fifteen-minute drive to the town centre police station. I sat in the allocated seat – behind the front passenger seat with Lauren by my side. I was becoming resigned to the unfolding events. As DC Hopkins advised the officer driving of the quickest route into town I noted both detectives in the car were younger than me. Where and how was the law of the land being upheld by people in their twenties? It might well have looked like I was pootling down to the pub with a few younger work colleagues.

DC Hopkins asked a handful of polite questions about the film and writing projects. I squeezed out a simple summary of the completed film and others in the pipeline. I didn't know her motivation for making such enquiries – to try to establish my professional background and how it related to the typical offender profile, or a genuine curiosity in the projects, or a roundabout way of soliciting more information before the solicitor advised me to shut up. Perhaps it was a way to relax me, to establish a rapport that might be more productive in interview? Or maybe she could even empathise with the shock an early morning visit from the police. Who knew?

Allowing me to sit 'uncuffed' in the car did not go unnoticed, but, then again, what did I know? My only experience of travelling in police vehicles came from television. As we approached the town centre, my thoughts turned to the fall-out of the day's events. Would my name be released to the Press? I asked. Would my name appear in the local papers? It filled me with horror that I was hours away from being thrust into such a maelstrom. Would I have to start alerting people (friends and former work colleagues) about my predicament before they saw it in the papers?

DC Hopkins suggested that the news would not be released at this stage. I did wonder whether the police would use the threat of releasing the news of my arrest as a lever for me to be 'cooperative'. We skipped through the traffic-restricted High Street and turned into the police station's drive.

Y1: 3. Police Station

We parked in a courtyard of police vehicles. DC Hopkins led me to a loading bay area while the other officers started to unload the cars of my computer equipment. (I wouldn't see any of it again for over three years.) We stopped outside a secure lift door and an intercom. DC Hopkins had her back turned to me (trusting, I thought) as she reported through the intercom that she had a man in custody to be interviewed. I appreciated the freedom to walk around in circles kicking loose gravel. The lift arrived and its doors opened. I stepped into the small space, the insides of which were split in two by a metal gate making the back of the lift, for want of a better word, 'a cage' the door of which hung open inviting me to enter. I waited for the detective's instruction to step inside the cage, but it never came. With me in a stunned state and with a rising sense of panic, we travelled in silence side by side up to the relevant floor.

The lift doors opened and we arrived at the custody desk. The forty-something male custody officer began booking me in: dates and times (9.30 in the morning) name and details (address, age, occupation) were handed over. I flinched as DC Hopkins informed the custody officer of the reason for arrest.

'Mr Anderson has been arrested on suspicion of downloading indecent images of children.'

The officer didn't bat an eyelid as he entered the arrest details on to the system remaining as chatty and indifferent as he had been when the custody booking had begun. It's just another day at the office for him, I concluded, or perhaps, I wondered, having been in my presence for two minutes, he realised there had been some mistake. He asked me if I had any medical conditions of which the police should be aware and if I had ever contemplated suicide. I didn't take this as an invitation to consider it, but it did make me wonder whether this was an appropriate question for someone not feeling at their best.

Not yet, I thought. 'No,' I mumbled.

My khaki shoulder bag and trouser pockets were emptied and all the contents logged. My wallet contained £170-00 in cash repaid to me by my brother over the weekend. I momentarily panicked and wondered if I had to explain what such a sum of money was doing in my wallet, but nothing was said. I signed off the list of belongings before being scanned by a metal detector and searched by another custody officer.

Nervous and not knowing how long I would be waiting before interview, I requested a lavatory visit. I was shown to a door in which a spy-hole was embedded halfway up the door. (A spy-hole not looking out of the lavatory, but looking inwards.) On entering I found no lock on the door and no sink, just a metal toilet bowl and a small cardboard box of toilet tissues. My business done, I exited and slipped around the corner to a sink embedded in the wall of the corridor. My momentary disappearance obviously triggered some alarm in DC Hopkins who suddenly appeared at the end of the corridor. Where was I going to go?

I was escorted to a nearby room for my fingerprints, DNA swab and photograph and left with a uniformed female officer. Where was my guard I thought? Couldn't I just run away? Or assault the uniformed female officer who was younger (albeit heavier) than me? Wasn't I, as a felon (was that the word?) not to be trusted? The officer pointed to a stool in the corner of the room positioned in front of a camera photo booth. As I took a seat, she announced she would be taking my DNA first. I wasn't sure of my rights, but having had grievances against the steady removal of civil liberties, I had always imagined I would protest violently if I had ever found myself in a position where my DNA was to be taken by the State to be held for eternity. Fully conscious I was failing to live up to the robust image of myself, I meekly asked the officer clerk whether I was obliged to give my DNA as I had objections to the 'initiative' and the erosion of civil liberties. The answer was 'yes', I was required to submit to a DNA swab, it was the law. The officer slid off her chair and approached me with a cotton bud. I would like to tell you that my resolve weakened, but that would suggest any semblance of strength was evident beforehand. I opened my mouth wide and my political and ethical convictions were swabbed away.

My fingerprints, palm-prints and side-palm prints followed – all scanned into a purpose-built scanner. I watched as she manipulated my image on the computer screen advising me to look straight into the lens. I wrestled with the dilemma of what expression one should adopt when one is being photographed for one's police record. I certainly didn't want to look criminal. A smile could make me look smug, unrepentant. I felt that I looked a bit like a stereotypical criminal anyway – shaven-headed and bland features that would probably scare babies. I did my best to look like a bewildered victim of a terrible misunderstanding, but never got to see (let alone approve) the image that might one day stare back from the printed page of a newspaper or flicker on a hundred million television and computer screens.

Now a fully registered criminal-in-waiting, I was shown out of the room. I assumed my next stop would be a holding room where I would stay until my solicitor arrived (which should be within the hour). I was escorted around a corner into a smaller corridor. I was met by a large, metal gate beyond which was a short corridor lined with heavy, metal doors – some of which hung open in a nonchalant welcome. This isn't right, I thought. Where's the waiting room or even the bench in the corridor outside the interview rooms? But no, my police escort stopped outside the door of a police cell.

'Remove your shoes and place them here,' he said pointing to the floor outside the cell.

I removed my reassuringly familiar suede boots and placed them outside the cell. They looked wholly out of place in the metal, clunky surroundings and mustard-coloured paint of the floor and walls. Presumably the removal of shoes was necessary to prevent me from hanging myself.

I don't recall the cliché of the clanging of the metal door behind me. It was a good-sized room. Protruding into one side of the cell was a shelf-like bed. A brown plastic mattress and pillow block sat propped up against the wall on the shelf-bed. Beside the door a functional, metal lavatory bowl was attached to the wall flushed by a button embedded in the plaster. A small box of lavatory tissues sat on the bowl. Otherwise the cell was empty. There was nothing in the cell that could be used as a weapon to harm oneself or another. Perhaps twelve feet above (and far out of reach), a square plastic light fitting was secured to the ceiling. At the end of a funnel-shaped shaft a four foot square glass skylight offered further illumination; similar to those found on pavements outside pubs or public buildings the skylight provided the only indication of the time of day. There were no windows. There was no clock.

A thick functional layer of orangey brown industrial paint adorned the walls. Black stencilled messages (aimed at the incarcerated) adorned the walls: 'CrimeStoppers – call in confidence – 0800 ...'; 'Taken into Consideration – you can ask the police/court to take other offences into consideration. This may help you when .....'.

Tucked high up in the corner of the cell above the door and looking straight at the shelf-bed was a security camera encased in a solid metal casing. I had seen a bank of TV monitors in the room behind the custody counter and acted on the assumption my every move was being recorded, but no fear, I assumed it would only be an hour or so before my solicitor arrived.

I took a seat on the shelf-bed and waited. Motionless, leaning forward with my elbows on my knees I stared at the floor turning things over in my mind. I would have a meeting with the solicitor and then we'd go into the formal police interview. What does one say? For what was I being held accountable? Would the police work against me and be crafty with the information they had? Where the hell did this all come from? Had I clicked on a link in a junk email or had a banner popped up somewhere? Whichever, I was in no doubt that what was going to happen in the next few hours would have a profound and unalterable effect on the following, say, forty to fifty years of my life and make any plans, hopes I had had since I was ten years old, wholly, wholly irrelevant. Plans and hopes for a career, travelling (visas) and relationships of all sorts would depend on the phrasing I adopted when answering questions in the interview. Even a pause (a result of my zoned-out state) as I considered a response to a question might have a detrimental effect on the forthcoming decades.

How honest should I be? Honest answers could be repackaged, re-spun and come back to haunt me cloaked in shades and hues unrecognisable to me. What if I made understandable mistakes when recalling dates, times, people? What if I made omissions – both intentional and unintentional – perhaps to protect friends and family, my privacy? What if I failed to mention something only for its relevance to become clearer much, much later in proceedings only for its effectiveness in my 'defence' to be impaired as a result?

Unable to sit still for long with such thoughts turning over in my head, I soon found myself walking around in circles around the cell, always in the same direction – clockwise. I did think it might be a good opportunity to do some stretching to work off the tension and expend the nervous energy, but I didn't really have the inclination. Besides, how would it look on the security camera? It might even be used against me in some way because, in the police's view, I was indifferent to the events unfolding? And so I walked.

After about twenty minutes or half-an-hour, I heard footsteps, the door opened and the custody officer appeared.

'Mr Anderson, your solicitor is on the phone.'

My heart sank. Just a telephone call? I thought I was going to meet the solicitor. I certainly wanted the solicitor in the interview with me. I wasn't sure I could do the interview on my own.

I was shown into a small room by the custody officer and given a phone handset. The woman on the other end of the line introduced herself as the appointed solicitor working with a group of criminal solicitors in Abingdon. I explained my shell-shock and disbelief, saying maybe I clicked on something in the past, but I wasn't the genuine (offending) article. She immediately warned me not to say anything further over the telephone – she didn't trust the police and suspected that the police would be listening into the call.

What? I thought. The police are good guys, they know they can't do that. Sensing my disbelief the solicitor said that the police wouldn't be able to use anything they heard – it would be inadmissible – but they would use it as 'intelligence' in their investigation. This was hardly reassuring.

The woman advised me that her colleague was in the police station assisting someone else, but he would pop in at some point to say hello. In the meantime I should be assured that someone from the company would arrive to represent me. The woman sounded nice on the phone – attentive, sympathetic and sharp – and I was hopeful that she herself would come to my assistance.

The phone call over, I eventually managed to get the attention of a passing officer and was escorted back to the police cell.

Then the waiting.

Waiting is manageable if one is able to track time, but when one is without any means to track the passage of time, it becomes bizarre, unreal. My watch and mobile telephone had been confiscated when I was booked in, there was no clock in the cell, no town bells chiming, no bells ringing. Placed in a small, plain room illuminated by artificial light while existing only in a state of panic, I was struggling to establish whether twenty minutes had passed or forty-five. Was forty-five minutes in fact ninety-minutes? Or even two or three hours?

As I was unable to sit still for long, I started walking around in circles until my legs got tired, at which point I sat down again. Whether my legs tired after twenty minutes or fifty, I could never tell.

Later, a police officer appeared at the small metal-flap embedded at chest height in the cell's door. She read out a list of unappetising-sounding microwave lunch options. None appealed.

'Do you have sandwiches?' I asked. I even offered to pay. I had visions of my stomach reacting to cheap microwave food and me not performing in the interview.

Nope, just microwave meals, I was informed.

I opted for the shepherd's pie.

After what seemed a good few hours, DC Hopkins' face appeared at the door-flap and informed me that the solicitor was still tied up in an interview, so she had phoned the solicitors and demanded that someone appear. She apologised for the delay and said it would probably be about twenty minutes before the solicitor arrived.

'What's the time?' I asked.

'Quarter to twelve,' she replied.

Okay, I thought. Once the solicitor was here, we'd have a fifteen-minute chat and then maybe an hour for the interview. I'd be out soon after 2.00 p.m., I thought. That's manageable.

Shortly afterwards my shepherd's pie arrived. I doubt a shepherd would have recognised it though. A shepherd certainly wouldn't have considered eating it – a hot, white plastic tray of brown sludge. A splodge of white cloudy sludge was floating in the middle of the brown sludge. It wouldn't have looked out of place in the metal receptacle in the corner of the cell. If I spilt the tray's contents on the floor, would I be accused of (even charged with) abusing the police's hospitality by not using the receptacle? My cries of 'It's the pie!' going unheeded.

Having not eaten properly the night before, skipping the scheduled cooked breakfast and not being allowed to bring food into the police station (for health and safety reasons), I thought I ought to eat something. I needed to ensure my brain had energy for the interview. So, sitting on the shelf-bed, hunched over the piping hot plastic tray, I used the suicide-proof plastic spoon (itself in danger of melting when it touched the steaming sludge) and forced myself to eat. Over an indiscernible period of time I managed to finish the tray's contents and felt a little better for it.

I had no idea how much time was passing. There was a little button sunk into the wall by the door which I guessed was connected to the custody counter, but I didn't want to trouble them. I walked in circles, my legs tired, I would sit then rise and start all over again. I said a little prayer that the interview would not be a complete horror and that I would struggle through the questions, giving answers while truthful and accurate would not give the police the ability to put a spin on them at a later date.

Y1: 4. The Interview

Eventually DC Hopkins opened the cell's door informing me that the duty solicitor was now available having finished another interview. I did worry that, having just finished defending one client, his mind wouldn't be focused on defending me, especially as it was getting quite late in the day. I learned that it was half-past three o'clock. I had been in the cell for nearly six hours.

I met the duty solicitor, Alex, by the booking-in counter just as he was signing off duties with his previous client. A tall, burly man, he immediately advised me that his colleague would arrive shortly (she was even in the station). He would hand me over responsibility for my interview to her, but in the meantime he would start the pre-interview solicitor chat.

I did wonder whether he knew the charges and whether this would affect his wish to defend me (who would, on such an allegation?). He seemed remarkably relaxed and matter-of-fact – busy perhaps, but indifferent to the reason for arrest (as did the police officers around the counter, including DC Hopkins). Was I the only one vexed by the nature of the day's events? There were no disgusted looks, no coldness, just everyday office banter between people who deal with each other every day. I was just another case on his conveyor belt of cases, but there was something reassuring about his emotionally detached manner.

Alex and I were shown into a consultation room. My mouth being dry (largely because of anxiety) I asked for a couple of plastic cups of water. Seated together in the room, he scanned the one page document from the police.

'They have nothing. I suggest you just decline to comment on all the questions they ask,' he said matter-of-factly.

I sought clarification.

'We just say 'no comment' to anything,' he replied.

This unsettled me, 'Isn't that what guilty people do?' I asked.

He shook his head. 'No.'

'Can I look at that?' I said nodding toward the piece of paper in his hand, still unsettled.

'Sure.'

The top half of the police's document listed administrative details: name, date and a statement saying that I had been arrested on suspicion of downloading indecent images. The lower half of the page was a section in which further details, evidence and reasoning could be listed. It was blank. Blank but for one line which had been CAPITALISED.

It was one line I uttered to my mother on the stairs that morning minutes after the arrival of the police – 'I might have had pop-ups and maybe I clicked something', but with capitalisation it read: 'I MIGHT HAVE HAD POP-UPS AND MAYBE I CLICKED SOMETHING' which to me was shouting the phrase and, unless it was the house style, lent it an importance that was wholly unwarranted.

There was no 'evidence' as such and no reference to the 'intelligence' that had triggered the visit in the first place. The backbone of the document seemed to be a passing speculative reference I had made trying to explain the madness of that morning, yet it looked to me (and anybody else reading it) that the words were 'an admission'. There was no reference to the discussion about the housemates, the reference to it being all 'adult stuff', my cooperation and the confusion I had expressed during the visit. It was a phrase taken out of context and wholly misleading. I was aghast.

'No, they have nothing. They're fishing,' said Alex. 'Say nothing.'

I expressed concerns that this might imply guilt, but again Alex assured me it didn't. After a few short minutes, the door opened and my designated solicitor, Alex's colleague, Alison, entered. After introductions and greetings, Alex left and Alison sat.

Alison was a similar age to myself. She was dressed in a trouser-suit and looked the part of a busy, no-nonsense solicitor familiar with (and even contemptuous of) the police. She reviewed the one-page document and, like Alex, said without a moment's hesitation, 'Say nothing – reply "no comment" to all questions'.

I expressed my dismay that the phrase had been taken out of context, but voiced my concern, even discomfort, at saying nothing in the police interview. After all I just wanted to sort it all out. Alison remained adamant and began briefing me on what would happen in the interview itself.

She said that the detective would start the tape then list those people who were present in the room and I would be expected to confirm my name. DC Lauren Hopkins would read out my rights whereupon she would ask me whether I understood at which point I should say 'no comment'. Alison asked me if I understood.

'Yes,' I said.

She shook her head. 'No, say "no comment",' she said, much like she would to an errant child.

Okay, I nodded.

'Do you want some water?'

'Yes, please,' I sighed, gratefully. In the circumstances my mouth was drying out every few minutes.

'No comment!' Alison spat, slapping both hands firmly on the table.

Okay, I nodded, meekly and wondering if I was going to get any more water.

'Say 'no comment' to everything they ask, because if you start answering some questions, but not others, then they will work it against us.'

Okay, noted. That makes things a little easier. 'How long would it last?'

'Forty-five minutes maybe.'

No doubt it would seem longer.

After a further discussion on what happens after the interview (namely, a little debriefing), I should then be bailed to reappear for another interview. And so we left the safety of the interview room and headed to the police custody desk.

We met DC Hopkins and her police colleague, PC Walters, who had been present at the house search that morning. After a request for more water we headed down a tight corridor to an interview room. Roughly square and without windows, it was more like a sound booth than an interview room. Pushed up against the wall there was a small table around which four chairs could just fit (with enough space for one person to move around). A double-decked tape recorder sat against the wall on the end of the table. The room was illuminated by a few spotlights in the ceiling that did little to offer warmth to the environment. The walls were covered with what appeared to be a sound absorbing material. I was directed to the far seat of the table (beside the wall) and opposite DC Hopkins. My solicitor, Alison, sat next to me.

DC Hopkins unwrapped tapes for the recording machine. PC Walters appeared with four paper cups of water (all for me) before taking a seat beside the arresting officer and opposite Alison. The mood was all smiles and cheerfulness. There was no sort of intimidation. It was all just routine for the other three individuals in the room. The audio tapes began to roll and DC Hopkins started by listing those present and asked me to confirm my name, which I did. I was asked whether I understood the charges and my rights which DC Hopkins had just repeated for the benefit of the tape. I glanced at Alison beside me, took a breath and said, 'I've been advised to say no comment'.

DC Hopkins and PC Walters noted my reply. I detected a hint of disappointment that they now knew how the interview was going to go. Alison, as promised in our meeting, confirmed for the tape the advice she had given to her client (me): '.... At the moment disclosure is inadequate for me to fully advise my client. I haven't been told when the incident occurred, why you think there are images on the computer, whether any images have been found on the computer or even whether you've looked at the computer .... So for this reason I'm now advising you not to answer any questions.'

DC Hopkins began reading from a thick, stapled set of papers – perhaps thirty pages – which was deeply unsettling. How long had they been compiling this dossier on me? But the questions started very broadly – my current home arrangements: who lived there; were there locks on the doors; did other people have access to my rooms; visitors and their access.

At this point my solicitor Alison chipped in with a question of her own.

'Just to reiterate: the reason my client is answering "no comment" is, as we've heard from the interview disclosure, the "suggestion" that my client downloaded indecent images of children when living at the previous address in Meadow Road. Would you like to explain why you are now asking him about Shrub Lane?'

'Yeah, well, I'll explain that to David,' DC Hopkins responded. 'The reason I'm asking questions about that address is because we are going to look at the computers to see if there are any indecent images on those computers. (Or if there is proof they have been present and been deleted.) Now, clearly you could have downloaded images at your current address as well. So that's why I need to know about where you live now and who has access to your room. Do you understand?'

I was not entirely convinced, but let it go. 'No comment.'

'Does your bedroom have a lock on the door?'

'No comment.' (There had never been a lock on any bedroom door.)

And so it continued. Then the same questions were repeated for my old residence in Meadow Road. Who lived there? Were there locks on the doors? Were there passwords on my computers? When did I buy the computer? Who had access to the computers? Software? Who installed it? Which Internet Service Provider? Any Internet chatroom use? Did I have a username profile for websites?

'No comment; no comment; no comment,' was my repeated response.

It slowly dawned that she was reading a pro forma list of questions. I waited for a specific question such as: Where was I on such-and-such a date? Do I know Mr X? How long have I known him? Your credit card ending in 1234, what do you use it for? Can you tell us how your email address came to be listed on this email circular? Did you sign up for this list?

But nothing. All very, very general. Every question asked in that room could be asked of any other person seated at that table (and even their extended families).

As the interview progressed, I didn't really have to think. As the minutes reached double figures then maybe half-an-hour, I almost stopped listening.

'No comment. No comment. No comment.'

It was almost easy, but I was never complacent or comfortable. My mouth was still dry and I was sipping water regularly working my way through the four cups of water. Out of water about thirty or forty minutes in, I turned to Alison, held up one of the four empty cups and tapped it politely with a questioning look. I daren't say anything.

'Do you think we can take some time to have another glass of water,' Alison said.

'Yeah, that's fine,' replied the detective, probably welcoming the break herself.

The tapes were turned off for five minutes, cups were refilled and tapes signed off. Things relaxed for a few minutes. I kept my mouth shut. Nothing was said about my responses. We resumed.

There was no clue as to the nature of the intelligence, nor any reason for the police visit to the house. The interview appeared to be moving to a close. DC Hopkins reminded me that I could answer the questions if I so choose to do so:

'Have you got any questions about the Caution? Have you got any questions so far about anything we've covered?'

However, glancing at Alison, I continued with my 'no comment' responses.

More general questions followed: Tell me about software; Do you defrag your hard drive? Do you use encryption? Your job role? Do you have any cause to research indecent images?

After a short while, Alison waded in, no doubt to exert a bit of pressure.

'Officer, have you actually interrogated the computer yet?'

'We haven't interrogated the computer.'

'You don't even know if there are any images?'

'We haven't interrogated the computer,' DC Hopkins repeated.

'Do you know if there are any indecent images on my client's computer at this stage?'

'No, I don't know.'

'So this is a fishing expedition?'

'It's not a fishing expedition.'

'On the disclosure you've given me and the fact that you don't even know there are indecent images on that computer, this is a fishing expedition.'

'That might be your opinion, but I'm not going to get into an argument about that now. We have intelligence that suggests David has downloaded images, indecent images of children and that's why we are interviewing you now,' she said turning to me. 'We're giving you an...'

'And this 'intelligence' ...,' Alison persisted.

'Can you just let me finish?'

'No, no, because ....'

'We're giving you an opportunity now ...'

'You ...'

'... to account for images we may find. We have good reason to believe you've downloaded images.'

Alison was having none of it.

'When you wish to share with us the 'good reason' that you believe that, then maybe my client will consider talking to you, but at this stage you've disclosed nothing. You're on a fishing expedition.'

I've never had women fight over me before. Contemporaries of mine might have found women fighting over them at wedding receptions, in pubs, at beach parties, in nightclubs, but me, no, it was Police Interview Room 2. I was unsure whether to be pleased for life's small mercies, or plain disappointed.

'I have no duty to disclose the intelligence to you, David. This is your first opportunity to make an account, okay? So, I'm going to return to the question that I asked ...'

'My advice to you is not to answer questions,' Alison chipped in.

'... that I asked and it's your choice whether or not to answer it. I'm not forcing you to say anything. When we analyse your computer which we think, we believe you've downloaded indecent images of children, do you believe we will find anything?'

'No comment.'

Then PC Walters, who had been sitting quietly for over forty minutes, offered his first question. 'Is it possible that whilst at the Meadow Road address and Shrub Lane anyone could have had access to your computer or computers?'

'You're asking my client to speculate,' snapped Alison. 'That's an unfair question. Don't answer that.'

'He is asking whether anyone had any access to it to your knowledge,' DC Hopkins added.

'That's a question that's been asked already, so it's irrelevant,' said Alison without missing a beat.

PC Walters rallied. 'Is it possible that you may have accidentally downloaded indecent images ...'

'You're asking my client to speculate, don't answer that question.'

And so it carried on for a few more minutes until I thought I could smell the end.

As the 'banter' wound down, I have to confess feeling a grudging respect for the British legal system. To sit in an interview room with agents of the State marshalled on the other side of the table, yet have beside me someone whom I had never met (and who knew virtually nothing about me) doing her best to knock six bells out of the police was a rather special thing. By myself, even as a grown man, I would have been struggling to manage the situation. So, my thinking went, hats off to all those who had come before me for haranguing, debating and agreeing laws and procedures which protected the interests of private citizens (at no cost to the arrested individual) when the unlimited resources of the State were squared up against them across said table. My guess is that if one were to be arrested in any part of the world, one could do a whole lot worse than being arrested in the UK.

'This is your first opportunity to talk to us,' DC Hopkins said. 'If you don't we may be back here talking about something else. But that is your choice.'

'Officer, you're inducing my client to answer questions, you know damn well he's coming back here because you haven't investigated the computers yet so he will be back her to answer further questions ... It is for you to prove beyond reasonable doubt that an offence has been committed. That's nearly 99%. So far you don't even know if there are any images on that computer. So before this turns into an unfair interview and an illegal interview I suggest you move on ..... .'

'Right okay.'

'You can roll your eyes at me ..'

'.. but you refer to an illegal interview and also ..'

'Well, it will become ...'

'Can you just ...'

'... aggressive if you keep asking these questions. It's a complete fishing expedition.'

After a few more minutes, it ended. It was, as Alison later noted, a list of questions she would 'certainly like to get her hands on'. I guessed the time to be approaching five o'clock. Leaving the room I was relieved and confused. I had expected more. The questions did not even indicate 'the nature' of what the police might have. I exited the room with the curious feeling that it was as if someone had just picked up the phone, called the police, given my name, a place, a date and made an allegation.

Alison and I retired to a consultation room.

'Well done,' she said. 'You did really well.'

Easy praise, I thought, I only had two words to repeat; but I was certainly relieved and even exhausted. Alison and I sat down and quickly deconstructed what little there was to deconstruct.

'And now what?' I asked.

'You'll be given bail and will be required to return for another interview when they have looked at our computer. We'll get our guys to look at your computer too.'

'And what do I do in the meantime?'

'Nothing,' Alison replied. 'There's nothing you can do.'

Y1: 5. Bailed

Judging by DC Hopkins' behaviour back at the custody desk, it didn't seem like a dead cert that I would be bailed. She seemed unsure, as if it wasn't in her gift, but after liaising with the custody officer she informed me that I was bailed to return four and a half months later (on 30 June).

The custody officer handed me a clear plastic bag of all my belongings and, at 5.15 p.m., Alison and I were escorted through a number of security doors, down the stairs and out onto the street. It was the rush hour and dark. I had been inside a windowless building since 9.30 in the morning. As we walked up to the town centre I pulled out the large plastic bag of my returned belongings and rifled through for my walkman radio, phone, wallet and keys.

'Put it away,' Alison gasped. 'People can see.'

It's come to that, I thought, that everyday passers-by could identify my new status (bailed criminal suspect) by the type of bag I used for my personal belongings. I asked Alison which people I should inform about my predicament.

'No one. If I were in your position I wouldn't tell anyone. Not even family. It carries such a stigma.'

Okay, well, my parents knew, they were present during the police visit which was, I concluded, in some ways a relief. A complete block on sharing it with anyone would be challenging. I had thought of calling my brother to go for a pint whereupon I would explain the events of the day, but Joseph, for all his good points was not the most discreet person. I had lost count of the times he had started a sentence with 'Don't tell anyone I told you this but ....'; 'I shouldn't tell you this but .....'; 'Promise you won't say anything but .....'.

I accepted Alison's advice, I wouldn't tell anyone, although I might have to account for the absence of my computers. I thanked her and we parted.

Standing in the busy town centre I phoned home and spoke to my parents. I explained the delay and ran through a summary of the interview and its non-specific questions. Generally speaking I was quite relieved. I relayed Alison's advice and we calmly discussed who should be informed of the day's events (and my new criminal status). I was of the mind that life, in the short term, would be easier if information was withheld, but it was only when my father mentioned the unequivocal support which would be forthcoming from my siblings, and more particularly my thirty-five year old baby sister, Maria, that I crumbled. My little sister had five children all under ten years old. Great kids, immaculately behaved, charming and sweet. Now an agency of the State was investigating an allegation that could threaten decades of trust within a family. Maria's priority would be to the safety and welfare of her children and the fact that my status should arguably be taken into account when I was in the room left me aghast and breathless. Who was responsible for this? Our discussions concluded with the agreement that we would follow Alison's advice not to inform friends and family.

My conversation with my father was briefly interrupted by the sighting of (and waving to) a former colleague who was heading home in the rush hour. Thinking I ought to say hello, I broke off the call and had a quick chat. Little did she know how things were really going, as we swapped everyday pleasantries. This was how things were going to be for while.

I could not face sitting on a public bus for the journey home. My head was too busy and I had been indoors all day. Besides the buses were slow and slower still from roadworks – trouble with tarmac apparently. Sitting amongst miserable faces staring gloomily out into the darkness is itself a form of imprisonment. An hour-plus walk might clear the head, burn off the energy and give me time to think. Removed from the world by my walkman radio and starting the long walk home, my thoughts soon turned to what had triggered the police visit and nature of the interview. I began to reflect on my days in a shared house and, in particular, my housemate's girlfriend who would come and stay for extended periods. A person who I thought I had shaken off.

Any memory of my time in the Meadow Road property was overshadowed by the German girlfriend, Anna Mannheim – the most vicious, spiteful, scheming woman I had ever met. My experiences with her had been why I had left the property and vowed never to share a house again. Mannheim certainly had used my computer and I remembered feeling most reluctant at complying with her request. By the time I had managed to talk them into moving out of the property, I had consulted with (and, to various degrees, enlisted support from) my brother, my neighbour, my parents, the landlord of the property, the City Council and a policewoman from Thames Valley Police. (More of which, later.)

As I trudged up the hill away from the city centre I was reasonably comfortable with the thought that I had kept a reasonable record of the trouble I had had with Mannheim in the house and could track down further supporting evidence. I thanked my lucky stars that, in anticipation of difficulties, I had kept a video diary recording the troubles in order to protect myself should difficulties later occur. All such records should be in the storage unit across the road.

Nevertheless, I tried to be open-minded and forced myself to consider other contenders, but it was a struggle. They would always be overshadowed by 'the one'.

I arrived home, ate and talked things through again with my parents. Having eaten in the evening I would have normally worked on the computer for a few hours, but I had to remind myself that all my equipment was bagged and tagged and now sitting in a police lock-up.

Y1: 6. The Next Day

Surprisingly I slept well. I woke up and all seemed normal but for a certain heaviness to my spirits. I found myself either just standing at the foot of the bed gazing into nothingness or moving very slowly back and forth between rooms. At times I felt my eyes welling up as my mind swung between a 'reality' and an insanity of disbelief. I suspected my wet and red eyes would remain just so all day, so best to keep a low profile. I wondered whether the constant nauseous feeling would ever leave me. No sooner had I considered it than I found myself hunched over a toilet bowl throwing up.

My room wasn't in too bad a state after the police's search of my belongings. I started to weakly shift though the stuff on my desk and came across a USB memory stick buried amongst various papers. Not just any memory stick, but a recent back-up of documentation. That's a relief, I thought, and waved it at my mother as she entered the room.

She asked me how I was; it worked. In my weakened state I crumbled and found myself offering to show what was on the USB stick. I stepped next door, plugged it into the eMac left by the police and opened its contents to show what (or rather, what wasn't) on the disk. My mother protested saying there was no need but between my blubs I noticed that she sat there looking at the stick's contents displayed on the screen – CVs, odd correspondence, the odd image related to my creative projects. Would I have to do this with everybody now – make a point of sharing the contents of any discs and storage devices?

I was grateful the USB stick had been left, but wondered about the competence of the police search. The previous day the alarm on my mobile phone had rung a few minutes after the police had arrived in full view of all the officers (at about 7.45 a.m.) as the officers started packing up my stuff. I switched the alarm off and stuck it in my pocket thinking nothing of it and even taking the phone with me to the police station. What was peculiar though was that the police saw fit to confiscate another (older) phone that I used as a back-up. Maybe they are not terribly well organised, I thought, which could work both ways.

On a normal day, I would sit down at the computer colour-correcting the movie and compile film paperwork. But ... I had no computers, so I revived the original plan for the previous day and decided to walk to the local shops for a cooked breakfast. During the fifteen-minute walk I found myself walking more slowly than I had ever done in my life. After all what was the rush? Everything had changed.

The events of the previous twenty-seven hours were going to affect every conceivable aspect of my life. Bizarrely, it was also rather humbling. All film and career options were now hanging by a frayed string over a deep, dark sea. I was now wholly and utterly at the mercy of events far beyond my sphere of influence. A life pretty much devoid of choice, self-determination. A different world from the one I had known since a boy when everything seemed possible. All the busyness that had preoccupied me up to the previous day had dissolved.

Bizarrely and sadly, I noted, I didn't even have the energy to miss it.

As I edged along the pavement mulling over this state of affairs, a black cat pattered down the front garden path of a bland, suburban home to my left and poked its head through the gate railings looking at the pavement in front of me. I stopped for a moment to let it slip through the gate and cross my path in the spirit of an old wives' tale, but it just stood there looked up at me and waited. It didn't move. Man and cat locked in a game of chicken. It was almost taunting me – I did not qualify for any good luck. Taking the hit, I sauntered on but turned around a few paces further down the pavement. The cat padded out through the gate and across the path behind me. Did that qualify as bad luck? Or just the absence of luck? To make matters worse I noted that its paws were white. It wasn't even fully black. Typical – even the non-fully-black cats weren't crossing my path.

The café had a few tables in the front window by the main service counter which were bathed in sunlight with a clear view of the street (with the street having a clear view of the tables). A gloomy dark corridor (in which a couple of small, poorly-lit tables were squeezed) led from the front of the café to the establishment's large back room which was bright but cheerless. Seated, I sipped my latte and tried to read an old newspaper I had brought just in case there were no papers available. I certainly didn't want to gaze into nothingness; the illusion of reading was much preferred. The cooked breakfast arrived – baked beans, mushrooms, two sausages, a single fried egg on toast. In spite of my nausea, I managed to put away the egg and toast. The beans weren't too difficult either. I couldn't face the mushrooms. Tried one, forced another, but I felt I was going to throw up, so I left the rest and half a sausage. A first for me. I would normally clear the plate. First the cat, then the cooked breakfast. I wouldn't have made a pretty sight – a hunched figure with a woolly hat pulled low over his eyes with one hand slowly shovelling beans into his mouth, the other hand over his eyes propping up his head, elbow on the table. Anybody with any sense of compassion seeing me might have felt compelled to enquire after my well-being, but I had chosen my gloomy corridor table well and I was undisturbed. I rose to my feet making sure an emotional spasm wasn't imminent and edged my way off the premises unnoticed, like a shadow thrown by a passing cloud.

Later that day I headed for the storage unit across the road. I was searching for the video recordings of my troubles in Meadow Road including my monologue to camera about my concerns. I moved slowly. Very slowly. Over the years I'd seen figures walking slowly about town with faces drained life. Now I was one of them. I quickly found a few tapes and headed home, plugged them into the television and skimmed through them but found only one relevant clip. Panicked, I returned to the unit and conducted a thorough search bringing home a whole handful of tapes. To my great relief, I found the footage I wanted and more besides. Now my most prized possessions, I would prioritise transferring them to VHS (I had no way to generate DVDs without a computer) and start logging their contents. I showed certain clips to my mother and father including sequences in which Mannheim left ranting messages on the house answerphone. I explained the background to video clips and my concerns that had prompted their recording in the first place (unpaid rent, theft and suspected benefit fraud). I didn't want anyone (including myself) to build up an assumption of her involvement, but it was only thing that made sense. My parents were unequivocal in their support of me; they were aware of the trouble I had had with my former co-tenant. Video session concluded, I threw my kit together and headed out for an evening of martial arts. A decent break from the events of the previous thirty-six hours, but I did start to think about when or how or if club colleagues should be informed of my predicament.

Y1: 7. February

The days became a week. Without a computer there was very little for me to do. Visiting a local gym to burn off some nervous energy I overheard a sport centre staff member talking on the phone as I entered the building.

'No we don't do CRB [Criminal Records Bureau] checks on people who use the gym,' he said.

I couldn't believe it. Normally I would have shaken my head in disbelief at the erosion of civil liberties, but now I couldn't raise a flicker of anything. Was this the future? Would my arrest appear on a CRB check? Or did it only apply to convictions?

The shock eased over the next week. The numbness lasted a little longer, but the fire and fight had been knocked out of me completely. When meeting my brother for coffee, I didn't mention anything. That was the agreed plan after all. Say nothing. Nothing could be done until 30 June. Four and a half months away.

Exercise was a good distraction. The karate club had known me for years and fortunately CRB checks did not appear to be on their radar. (Or if it had been practice, I had missed it, just like much else referring to criminality before my arrest.) Although I understood the need for teachers and instructors to submit to such checks, it was noted in the Press that attendees of courses (for instance in Further Education) were not required to submit to checks. Nevertheless, when my instructor looked troubled and preoccupied on one particular occasion, I suddenly wondered whether the police had approached him and advised him of the bail status of a club member. Taking place immediately before the senior class there was a 'family' session that I usually skipped unless they asked for my help. Now, I thought, I decided I would avoid the family sessions altogether. (Why? Because the thought that there could be any suggestion that I had an ulterior motive made me feel sick.)

The days following the arrest I made a point of getting out of the house – going to the cinema and playing squash with my long-standing squash buddy, Ryan.

'How's your week been?' he asked, as he must have done every week for the previous ten years.

'Fine,' was the only possible reply.

Never had I thought that I would spend a birthday (39 years old) on police bail. I had received a handful of cards and one package – a small box of dark chocolates from an old work colleague, Mel. She had emailed me earlier in the week asking how things were going and for a new postal address. Her email, card and chocolates served only as a reminder that there was another phase yet to endure. What would these people think? Would they ever know? How would they know? Via the Press? Word-of-mouth? Would I have to tell Mel and others in person? Would it change things? How? Would they skip sending birthday cards and gently withdraw? Or would they be understanding and defer judgement?

Y1: 8. March, April, May, June

The purpose of taking the career-break-sabbatical had been to focus on the film options. In the months leading up to the police visit I had attended various courses and became a fully qualified 'Apple Pro' in Final Cut Pro editing software. I had edited together a show-reel of my short and feature-length films and the week before the police visit I had been registering with agencies with a view to working freelance. I sent CVs to colleagues and contacts for whom I had already done some video editing as part of my job. Now that the film had gone, I had not an ounce of creativity in me, coupled with the fact that I might find myself in a criminal court in a matter of months which would throw any freelance job offers out the window. I therefore desisted from any further self-promotion or registration with agencies. Therefore it was a surprise in April to receive an email from my former employer asking me to film (and therefore edit) a few lectures. My efforts pre-arrest to promote myself had borne fruit. I would be paid as a freelancer. It was my first offer of work.

The email sat in my inbox and I looked at it for a day, then another, then another. I had no means to deliver edited footage. I did consider arranging a bank loan to purchase a whole new suite of editing equipment, but any money I made would not make a dent in the loan. I never replied to the email.

With no film activity and no income, I was therefore obliged to consider returning to paid employment in a non-creative context. I did submit a few speculative applications for administrative posts in creative organisations, but times were difficult post-2008 credit crunch and I wasn't successful. Thus my attention turned to work I had hoped I had left behind – administrative posts in higher education, but there were difficulties there too. Some jobs were simply off-limits – they required (or might have required) a Criminal Records Bureau (CRB) check, which I could do without.

On job applications' 'How to apply' instructions, I would often come across a request that had flitted across my mind in the previous few weeks: 'Have you ever held convictions....' or referred to 'criminal proceedings'? I certainly wasn't going to put the details of my predicament down on paper. After all I didn't know where the information would end up.

'It's a sign,' my mother would say, 'stick with the creative stuff. You're not meant to go back to that kind of work.'

I ended up emailing solicitor Alison to ask about my status in terms of employment applications. Were there currently 'criminal proceedings' against me or would that come later, after a charge? I had a reply a day or so later:

> *David, to me proceedings mean "before a court".*
> *At the moment you are simply under suspicion*
> *and you have not been charged with an offence.*
> *Therefore I interpret it to mean that proceedings*
> *haven't begun yet. I will look it up and email you*
> *by the end of the day if I am wrong. If you don't*
> *hear from me then I am right!*

I didn't hear from her.

My understanding was that my arrest shouldn't show up on the standard CRB check – only convictions or possibly charges, but one never knew and so I never felt it was worth the risk. It could possibly appear on the 'enhanced CRB check'. In the end I applied for nearly fifty jobs before I was short-listed for a local administrative job in higher education.

Aside from the distractions and applying for jobs, I felt obliged to educate myself about the predicament I was facing. Unpleasant though it was, I made a point about researching the law, other criminal cases and police practice. Firstly, the options open to the police.

I researched the law and learnt the difference between the charges 'making' and 'possessing' indecent images. My inexpert legal understanding suggested the 'making' of an image did not require 'taking a photograph' (as one might think) but could mean merely 'making it appear' on a computer screen (i.e. presumably opening a file). 'Possessing' images seemed to mean the knowledge of the image(s) existence on a computer (which might not involve the 'making' of the image on a computer screen). Possession did not require 'making'. I read around various articles and comments on forums including those from disgruntled people who had felt badgered into accepting cautions for offences (for which they did not feel responsible) only to regret it at a later date. Just conducting the simple research made me feel ill, so I soon dropped it adopting the view I would revisit the matter only if circumstances required it.

Nevertheless, I soon came across newspaper articles which led me to reports of a 'blog' by an anonymous writer called 'Nightjack' about life in the police force. The blogger was eventually 'outed' by *The Times* newspaper as a police detective with the Lancashire Constabulary. For years Nightjack had blogged about life as a Detective Constable (DC – the same rank as my arresting officer, Lauren Hopkins). The blog had been eventually deleted (police officers are not permitted to express opinions), but some postings survived on the Internet in different forms including the postings giving advice to 'decent people' about what to do if they are arrested. There was advice under headings such as: Complain First Always; Make a Counter Allegation; Claim Suicidal Thoughts; Actively Complain About Every Officer and Everything They Do, amongst others, but a number of sections were particularly telling:

> ***Never explain to the Police****: If the Police arrive
> to lock you up, say nothing. You are a decent
> person and you may think that reasoning with the
> Police will help. "If I can only explain, they will*

*realise it is all a horrible mistake and go away".
Wrong. We do want to talk to you on tape in an
interview room but that comes later. All you are
doing by trying to explain is digging yourself
further in. We call that stuff a significant
statement and we love it. Decent folk can't help
themselves, they think that they can talk their way
out. Wrong.*

Admit Nothing*: To do anything more than lock
you up for a few hours we need to prove a case.
The easiest route to that is your admission.
Without it, our case may be a lot weaker, maybe
not enough to charge you with. In any case, it is
always worth finding out exactly how damning the
evidence is before you fall on your sword. So
don't do the decent and honourable thing and
admit what you have done. Don't even deny it or
try to give your side of the story. Just say nothing.
No confession and [the] CPS [Criminal
Prosecution Service] are on the back foot
already. They foresee a trial. They fear a trial.
They are looking for any excuse to send you home
free.*

Keep your mouth shut*: Say as little as possible to
us. At the custody office desk a Sergeant will ask
you some questions. It is safe to answer these. For
the rest of the time, say nothing.*

Claim Suicidal Thoughts: *A debatable one this. Claiming to be thinking about topping yourself has several benefits. If you can keep it up, it might just bump up any compensation payable later. On the other hand you may find yourself in a paper suit with someone watching your every move.*

Always, always, always have a solicitor: *Duh. No brainer this one. Unless you know 100% for sure that your mate the solicitor does criminal law and is good at it, ask for the Duty Solicitor. They certainly do criminal law and they are good at it. Then listen to what the solicitor says and do it. Their job is to get you off without the Cops or CPS laying a glove on you if at all possible. It is what they get paid for. They are free to you. There is no down side. Now decent folks think it makes them look like they have something to hide if they ask for a solicitor. Irrelevant. Going into an interview without a solicitor is like taking a walk in Tottenham with a big gold Rolex. Bad things are very likely to happen to you. I wouldn't do it and I interview people for a living.*

Show no respect to the legal system or anybody working in it: *You think that if you are difficult, unpleasant, sneering, uncooperative and rude things will go badly for you and you will be in more trouble. No sirree Bob. It seems that in fact the worse you are, the easier things will go for you if, horror of horrors, you do end up convicted.*

*Remember to fake a drink problem if you haven't
developed one as a result of dealing with us
already. Magistrates and Judges do seem to like
the idea that you are basically good but the
naughty alcohol made you do it. They treat you
better. Crazy I know but true.*

*So there you go, basically anything you try and do
because you are decent and straightforward hurts
you badly. Act like an habitual, professional,
lifestyle criminal and chances are you will walk
away relatively unscathed. Copy the bad guys, it's
what they do for a living.*

It was both reassuring and unsettling. It was reassuring
that it matched what others familiar with the police were
saying; it was unsettling that this was a police detective talking.

Inevitably, my thoughts during this time also turned to my
experience in Meadow Road. I had moved into the two-
bedroom property in 2000 and, with the landlord's blessing I
had organised a succession of co-tenants. I had had a young
couple (who moved away and got married); then a woman (who
moved to London for a course); then a man (who moved north
for a job); then Ian Linklee (and Mannheim) for four years
(neither of whom worked); then (briefly) a man, before I moved
out myself. Broadly speaking all tenants had been fine but for
Linklee and his regular visiting girlfriend, Mannheim.

Without a computer, without 'employment' of any sort,
my mind was left to retrace thoughts, reflections and haul out
little memories of life in Meadow Road. I was grateful that I
had made a video diary of the difficulties with Mannheim and

Linklee for use at a later date should difficulties arise (including countering any malicious allegations from them – something I was aware she had done to others). I recalled that on one occasion early in the video diary period I felt too tired to undertake the recording. It was late at night, I had to cue up a tape, charge a battery and I stood at the corner of my bed on the verge packing my equipment away and going to bed. Just as I made the decision to forget it and head to bed, a 'voice' or sense or presence (and something I felt was separate to my inner conscience), said: 'do it; you don't know just how it might be of use at a later date'. Such was the clarity of the 'message', I rigged up the tape and camera, had a late night and recorded footage of the house and my concerns.

The seized computer had not been password-protected and had been used by others during the eight year period that it had sat on my desk. In fact Mannheim herself had used it on occasion even while I was in the house. What I feared was that she had been using it in my absence. Both Mannheim and Linklee were unemployed and when in town, spent most of their time in the house. Being a working man regularly engaging in sport, my hours in the house had been limited.

One day lying on the bed and looking out the window a thought occurred to me that first appeared as an indifferent memory of a time spent sitting at a computer in Meadow Road, but very soon developed into a real and very relevant concern. The 2000s was a grand time for scammers and spammers. My email accounts would often be flooded with unwanted emails and it was a struggle to filter, block and delete them. Similarly, there would be pop-up windows promoting gambling opportunities, pharmaceutical drugs, saucy pictures or other. There would also be pop-ups masquerading as messages from my computer system saying there was a problem and I should click to download virus protection. I was sufficiently computer-

and-Internet-savvy to treat all such messages with caution and even take care exiting the pop-up window itself, for even clicking an 'exit' or 'no' button might well be the crafty way to get the computer user to download a virus or similarly unwanted program. These pop-up 'operating system' windows were almost always in MS Windows format, so, being a user of a Mac computer, I knew they were bogus.

However, as I gazed out the window thinking back to such times, I did distinctly recall one (or rather two) occasions that had been different. On one occasion a pop-up window appeared announcing that someone was 'trying to gain control of the computer' and gave me an option (or two) to deal with it. What was noteworthy was that the pop-up window was not only in a Mac OS format and design but similar to OS9 (not the current OSX). At the time I interpreted this as coming from deep within the computer's Operating System. I had had similar OS9 windows when I was configuring the computer for video-editing, so I was confident it was a genuine message. When I do not fully understand the implication of the actions proposed, I follow the course of action recommended by the computer (which I could not recall several years later) – possibly 'disconnect the Internet', 'block the impostor' or other. I recalled the incident distinctly, because it happened again in such a way that I connected the two occurrences and speculated that it was a teenager from, for instance, the Ukraine or China, trying to access my bank details or other. The two occurrences happened in a timeframe that had led me to believe it was the same 'individual'. In retrospect, I estimated the two occurrences had been five days to five weeks apart.

As I reflected on these events, there were two things of note: firstly, the pop-up windows had not happened since that time (to my knowledge), so I was wrong to assume it would become the norm, far from it. Secondly, I had been sitting at the computer to witness the pop-up events. What concerned me was the possibility that similar 'windows of warning' had appeared but I had been out of the room at the time and been unable to initiate a defence. As my mind swirled about on my crazy predicament, I thought, surely not? Even though the timing matched, surely those pop-ups were not connected to Mannheim? Nevertheless, I made a mental note to ensure that if some dubious material was found on my computer in some form, I should give serious consideration to the relevance of those pop-up windows during my tenancy.

Similarly my mind skipped through all the possible permutations of how legal proceedings would develop. I reflected on how the interview questions might stray from matters relating to the computer and its use to other areas of my life including other people – family and friends. Questions not so much to assist the police in their investigation but to create a climate of difficulty and pressure in the interview. How does one answer questions to respect and protect the privacy of others, let alone oneself?

Courtroom scenarios even worked their way into my imaginings. Needless to say Mannheim and Linklee were present in all of them. I would refer to the difficulties and share video clips supporting my assertions. Similarly I could call upon the landlord and others to bear witness to my difficulties – I fortunately had printouts of emails supporting such. The one thing I did not have was the confirmation of my interaction with Thames Valley Police during the Linklee-Mannheim tenancy. I suspected I had thrown away the Post-it note or envelope onto which I had written the name of the police officer I had been liaising with. I had a 'PC White' in my head, but felt confident that recordings of the phone calls could be retrieved from any police archive. Nevertheless, there would be no harm in establishing exactly when I had made the calls and making it possible to point to a telephone bill during (any) trial.

The trouble was, I didn't have any mobile telephone bills for the period. I had been on a Pay-As-You-Go contact that did not generate paper invoices and records, however I was confident the phone company records would be pretty comprehensive. After answering bail on 30 June I could direct the police to checking my phone records (of course, only if the police saw fit to continue with their investigation). So, because it could wait, it waited. I was aware that my imagination might run away with itself, so was I keen to keep it in check. If I had learnt anything, it was that however much one thought through all the possibilities there would always be surprises. Besides, I reassured myself, it would all blow over soon.

When I had first been bailed the second interview felt very far away, but ever so slowly, the first month (and then six weeks) dissolved away. Soon I was halfway through the bail period. Then, with ever-increasing speed, 30 June was a month away. Then two and a half weeks. Then ten days away.

What was more important than anything in the last week was 'Distraction' (with a capital 'D') largely in the form of carefully chosen DVDs. *The West Wing* had been a god-send, but the seven series had only lasted until early May. Toby, CJ, Josh, Leo and, of course, President Bartlett had all become dear friends. Having been a fan of the animated Pixar films I rented the film *Cars*. It did not disappoint. In fact it worked surprisingly well at raising my spirits and reminding me of the need to have some perspective. The impending interview was not only beginning to overwhelm my already 'busy head', but I was all too aware of the fallout following 30 June. Again, there was not one aspect of my life that the event wouldn't affect (or rather 'poison') – in the short, medium and long term. The film delivered the upbeat chirpiness of a Pixar film charting the young 'rookie' race-car's pursuit of the Piston Cup against the long-standing champion and another crafty contender. Crossing America to reach California for the season's final race, the rookie Lightening McQueen gets lost and ends up being trapped in Radiator Springs, a 'hick' town on Route 66 that had died a slow death after the construction of the Interstate. Spending four days in the slow lane, he learns about life and how unexpected, even unwelcome, events can be informative and educational leading to all sorts of new opportunities. The song over the end titles ('Find Yourself' by Brad Paisley) hit the mark and brought home that my predicament ought to be treated as a life experience.

Y1: 9. Answering Bail

On the Friday before the Tuesday 30 June interview I spoke to one of my solicitors, Alex. I expressed my apprehension about the upcoming interview, but he reiterated that it was up to the police to make the case against me, to prove that I had done what they said I had done. There was, he said, nothing I could do in preparation for the interview. It was a matter of wait and see. His own role at this stage was purely reactive. In fact his colleague, Alison Walcott, had also suggested after the initial interview that the strategy in the second interview might well be to say nothing again (i.e. "no comment"). This had surprised me at the time, but having reviewed articles in papers and the Internet (including 'Nightjack') in the weeks leading up to my first visit to the police station since my arrest, I was prepared to say nothing.

On my way to the station I found myself (figuratively) shaking my head in disbelief that the four and a half months had passed. Once, '30 June' had been a mythical date originating from one sheet of A4 created on a day of craziness deep inside an agency of State. It was a date against which almost every task had to be checked and evaluated: job applications, interviews, interaction with family members and friends, holidays. Not only did the date of 30 June split the year in two exactly, I anticipated that it might even split my life in two. Thirty-nine years, a clean sheet; then 'xx' years of 'something else'. That said, I knew that the date that had had a hold over me for every moment during the previous 130 days would lose its grip on me fifteen hours later.

With no inkling as to what would happen at 10.00 a.m. my head ran through various scenarios. My troubles could finish for good (no charge – it was all a terrible mistake and I could breathe a sigh of relief), or there could be an interview, then a criminal charge and a walk across the road to the Courthouse. Would it be that day? By midday? Or maybe 120 minutes later? Or would I be bailed to reappear a few weeks later?

Having arrived in the police station I introduced myself to the officer staffing the reception counter and was told to take a seat and wait. My solicitor Alex soon appeared. I introduced myself to him saying I had a few questions for him before we entered the station proper.

'Do you want to speak in here?' he asked motioning to the reception area. No doubt I look confused because he continued. 'There might be microphones. The police might be recording the conversation.'

What? WTF?

'No, it's okay,' I replied, masking my disbelief. Nevertheless, I lowered my voice as I sought his view on the return of (any) computer equipment and on the source of the 'intelligence' that had triggered the police visit. Could it be a tip-off? Malicious?

Alex was non-committal.

After a short wait a young woman appeared at the reception counter. Was it DC Lauren Hopkins, my arresting officer? I might not have recognised her in any other situation. I hadn't seen her for nearly five months and the day we had met each other I had been quite fraught

'David?' I heard her say looking in my direction.

'Yes?'

I rose to my feet and approached the counter. I noted that my solicitor remained seated behind me. I thought he was supposed to be, if not by my side at all times, in front of me punching the living daylights out of the coppers.

'You've been re-bailed. We're not ready to continue at this stage. They are still looking at the equipment.'

Any sense of relief would not have been apparent to anybody looking at my ashen features.

'I'm not looking after your case anymore,' she continued. 'I've passed it on to a colleague, DC Chris Woods.'

She handed me a brown A5 envelope. Opening it I found that I had been re-bailed to appear at the police station on Monday 31 August, two whole months away.

I relaxed. DC Hopkins seemed completely indifferent as she turned and disappeared back into the depths of the station. I turned to Alex.

'Can I buy you a coffee?' I asked, keen to speak to someone about my predicament. I hadn't had a proper conversation with anyone for months.

'Sure.'

Across the road at 10.05 a.m. in a coffee house (fortunately empty on a weekday morning), Alex and I sat near the window (and as far away from the manned service counter as possible). During our twenty-minute conversation explaining the situation as I saw it, I felt my whole body sigh and relax. As I had said to him on the day of my arrest, I had viewed a bit of standard porn at intervals over the years, but unless I was going crazy, I hadn't come across anything remotely explosive. I explained that the computer was not password-protected, used by others (including housemates), in a house with no lockable internal doors and I had had considerable difficulties with the housemates at the time. If the 'intelligence' had been human in origin, there was a leading contender – a person about whom I had spoken to the police at the time should there be difficulties when (or after) the co-tenants moved out.

I wasn't sure that Alex bought my story. Perhaps I was just another client flailing around blaming the world about them. Although a little disappointed, I reasoned that I wouldn't want a solicitor who was wholly un-cynical of his client. It just meant I had to 'up my game' (assuming that was the game I wanted to play). Nevertheless, he said that in light of my words there was a 60-70% chance it would be all dropped and the re-bailing was a good sign. The delay suggested that I was not a priority and the police's information might be limited.

Y1: 10. July, August, September

As a 'free man' I started a new job in mid-July, but it did not stop me from having visions of Mannheim phoning the department to make an allegation or reporting to my new employers that I was on bail for an unsavoury crime. Thus, in the first few months, I could not entirely relax for there was always the possibility of being called into a manager's office for a painful, painful conversation.

I was unable to move forward. All my computer equipment and film material was still sitting in a police lock-up. 'Prospects' are arguably fiction, but when one is even deprived the fiction of prospects, what is left?

On the second occasion of answering bail (Bank Holiday Monday: Days on Bail – 195) the police station itself was empty as if it was, er, a holiday (unlike my previous visit two months earlier). Five minutes before my designated time to answer bail (and nearly seven months after my arrest), I identified myself to the officer manning the reception counter. There was no sign of my solicitor, Alex. I watched the officer phone through my details upstairs. I took a seat and waited.

There was one door to the left of the main reception counter, which I assumed to be the one route into the building for visitors such as myself. I watched it, my ears alert to any suggestion that there was movement on the other side – a door to my life-in-waiting. Hearing noises and some male voices I braced myself for the start of the something new. At least I should have an answer to the question – 'what's this all about?' The response 'I can't tell you that' should now be redundant, surely? By the end of the day I would have had a fair idea of how deep and frequent my laughter would be in the forthcoming years.

The noises and voices behind the door receded whereupon a plain-clothed woman suddenly appeared behind the reception counter.

'David Anderson?'

I stood and approached the counter. I always assumed 'Chris Woods' was 'Christopher' and not 'Christine'.

'I don't know why you were booked to return on a Bank Holiday. It is an oversight on our part, it seems. No-one's here,' the woman said.

'Oh right,' I replied, not knowing to be angry, a bit annoyed, or relieved, or disappointed or something else. The thought of enduring the wait all over again would hit me later, no doubt.

'Chris will call you tomorrow'.

'I did have to be here?' I asked.

I wanted to be sure that I hadn't done something wrong. Or, at the very least, I didn't want the police thinking I had erred in some way. I was unable to check the re-bail notice itself as I had made a point of not carrying the document around with me in case it fell out the bag or if I was knocked over by a bus and passing Good Samaritans morphed into Worthy Assassins.

'Oh yeah,' the woman replied. 'but it's a Bank Holiday. An oversight on our part.'

Could I give her an earful? Best not, I concluded. I noticed the papers she had with her – just like the re-bail notice DC Lauren Hopkins had issued me when I was re-bailed in June, two months earlier.

'Do you have a bit of paper for me?' I asked.

The woman looked blank.

'I was given a bit of paper last time.'

'No, Chris will call you tomorrow and arrange a convenient time to meet.'

I learnt later that I had been re-bailed to 20 October– a further seven weeks. As had become habit, I kept checking on local and national newspaper stories about people arrested and prosecuted. One local man had been arrested in February (like me) but had been tried and imprisoned by September. Others had been arrested in the spring – several months after me – their cases investigated, charged and prosecuted by late summer. All within three, four or five months. Here I was approaching seven months and nobody had told me anything. Perhaps I ought to be grateful, I thought. There were no awkward conversations at work required. I was unable to confirm a holiday, but it did not stop me researching trips. I tried to take some solace in the fact that I was at least banking cash. In time, my frustrations turned to resolve. Even if events did take a nasty turn, it normally took a few months to schedule a trial, so in September I booked a walking holiday in Nepal in mid-December.

The same resolve determined that I should take the initiative with some of my defence-preparation and I decided to go ahead and approach my mobile phone provider (Orange) for the phone records of nearly three years earlier. I emailed:

> *I had an mobile Pay-as-You-Go account a few years ago and I may need to access my phone records for a legal matter. .... I made various phone calls to the police from my mobile and may need to refer to them in a court of law. How do I go about getting those records? I should be grateful for your urgent attention to this matter, as I have a meeting with a solicitor next week.*
> *... ....*

The reply was swift:

> *Thank you for your email regarding your enquiry. I am sorry to learn you require your mobile phone records for an old Pay As You Go account. Please find enclosed address, to which you will need to write requesting this information...*

I was encouraged. At least I could show that I had made the effort putting a defence case together and any claim I made later in a police interview could not be dismissed as retrospective and desperate. I could prove that I had drawn the matter of my troubles to the attention of the authorities during my Meadow Road tenancy. Any sense of encouragement did not last, however. The following day I received a follow-up email from a different Orange employee:

> *Unfortunately, after reading your previous email the details you were given were not entirely correct as you mentioned you need the details for legal reasons. In order to obtain this information you will need a legal representative to request this information by writing to the following address: Security Assurance and Business Support .... Unfortunately, we cannot guarantee that we have all records for the past 2 years. I hope this information is useful to you and sorry for any inconvenience caused.*

Y1: 11. October, November

In October, having run through a similar routine, I was re-bailed again and after a bit of to-and-fro the date on which I was required to answer bail was 8 December. Once I had digested the delay, the reaction of my mind and body varied. At times I was indifferent, at other times edgy, but often times I was angry. How could a person be kept on tenterhooks like this with no information as to the reason for the police visit and the confiscation of a livelihood? I was at a loss as to why the police could not get their act together. I became more and more concerned about the lack of organisation and human failings. Constantly reviewing newspaper reports, I began to wonder about the effectiveness of the police.

The news media reported on Criminal Records Bureau (CRB) checks. Authors invited into schools (presumably for no fee) protested that they had to pay money to be checked. Members of the public phoned radio shows saying 'you couldn't be too careful'. There were reports of a policewoman breaking the law for looking after a friend's children. In another part of the country parents had been advised that they could not enter a children's play area in a park with their own children because they (the parents) hadn't been CRB-cleared to supervise their own off-spring. Only the CRB-cleared Council warden staff could supervise the children in the park. The parents would have to watch from behind a fence. The logic puzzled me. Was the Council afraid the parents would venture into a park to abuse their children in public (rather than at home) or kidnap their own children from the park and take them back to their own home to abuse? Had anyone studied the risk to children's mental health of denying interaction between a parent and child and/or introducing (perhaps albeit subconscious) distrust in the parent-child relationship?

Before my arrest I had been entertaining the idea of a visit to the United States with the completed film to set up meetings and develop relationships. Looking at the US visa application website, applicants needed to disclose whether they had been arrested for (note, not just 'convicted' of) a 'crime involving moral turpitude' (CIMT) which included pretty much everything including downloading indecent images. I was aware that the longer my predicament continued, the more it might take root.

Y1: 12. Answering Bail, December

Tuesday 8 December arrived. (Days on bail: 294.) Two weeks earlier the investigating officer DC Woods hadn't had news from the computer technicians, so I was half-expecting to be re-bailed again (which would not be unwelcome, I did not want to upset my plans for hiking in the Nepal four days later).

I entered the police station five minutes before the appointed time (four o'clock) wearing several additional T-Shirts and carrying a jumper into my shoulder bag just in case – I didn't want to shiver in any interview. I gave my name to the woman at reception saying that I had a meeting with DC Woods. She disappeared into the back office and made a phone call. Watching her reactions through the glass wall it appeared that the person on the other end of the line was confused. The receptionist returned.

'He's not expecting you, but he's coming down,' she said.

Wow, a good sign? I thought to myself. It was obviously not on DC Woods' mind. I would be sent away and I could enjoy Nepal. A few minutes later after several passers-by and false alarms, a man I didn't recognise appeared at the counter.

'Mr Anderson?'

'Yes?'

I stepped forward. He identified himself as someone unknown to me and from a different department unrelated to my case and predicament.

'I'm here for DC Chris Woods? For a 4.00 o'clock appointment,' I said.

The man sighed, shrugged and turned to the officer on reception to explain that she had made an error. Alone again, I returned to my seat. Here we go again, I thought, as I watched the woman officer retire again to the back office to make another phone call. There was obviously no brown A5 envelope waiting for me behind the desk this time. (Unless she really was useless. One could but hope.)

She returned and informed me that he was coming down. To personally issue me with the re-bail notice? The personal touch was nice, but not necessary.

After a few more minutes the woman desk officer reappeared.

'Mr Anderson, there is a queue booking in at the desk, so Simon will be down shortly.'

'It's DC Chris Woods,' I said, thinking, hoping, assuming she had more mistakes up her sleeve.

'Yes, Simon Caine is his partner,' she replied.

I gave a nod of thanks. There were two of them?

More minutes passed and my innards slowly sank. Something was afoot. I was not being sent away. Or if I was, they were labouring the process.

A tall, thirty-something professional man appeared and explained to me that my solicitor was on his way, consequently there would be a thirty-minute delay. Again, I nodded and took it in. Like swallowing a shock pill, it was slowly taking effect. Sounds like it is on, I thought. After nine and a half months. Holy cow.

I stepped outside the police station to phone home and explain developments. At 4.20 p.m. on a mid-December day, it was dark and cold. The day had become threatening; life has these tough moments, I noted. I returned to the cold, stark illumination of the police reception waiting area and started making notes to kill time.

At 4.50 p.m. another officer appeared behind the reception counter. I recognised him from the home visit in February, but I soon learnt it was not Chris Woods, but his partner, Simon Caine. Informed that DC Woods was heading back to the station I was advised that it would be better for me to remain waiting in the police reception which was more comfortable than waiting outside the exterior lift that led up to the booking-in area. Apparently, there was 'a whole load of other prisoners' waiting to be booked in.

WTF? "Prisoners"?

'How long will it take?' I asked, politely.

'I don't know,' DC Caine replied.

'Will it be over by seven o'clock?' I asked, thinking of the Spanish language class I had scheduled around the corner.

'Unlikely,' he said, looking at his watch. 'Why do you have something? You can make some phone calls.'

'I have a class round the corner at 7.00 p.m.'

'I think it is unlikely we'll be over by 7.00 p.m. The clock is ticking on you.'

I didn't understand what the 'clock ticking on you' meant, but that did not prevent me from politely nodding before obediently sitting and make some more notes. I started to reflect on the implications for the next 96 hours: would it be a problem for Nepal?

The hands on the reception clock moved just past five o'clock whereupon the door, on which I had maintained a beady eye for the previous hour, opened. A plain-clothed man (average height, short-hair) stood in the doorway. His expression gave nothing away. I didn't recognise him – he certainly wasn't one of the officers who had visited the house on the day of my arrest.

The man called my name. I rose and approached him as he stood with his back to the door keeping it open. He was almost certainly younger than me – perhaps 30 years of age. I assumed he was doing the same to me – sizing me up for the first time.

I followed DC Woods into the station and through a network of offices until we reached the courtyard at the back of the station. Once again I was intrigued to see that he was content to escort me through the premises with his back turned. Didn't it occur to him that I could clobber him on the back of the head and make a run for it? As we walked he also reported that it had been better for me to wait in reception as colleagues were booking in lots of other prisoners. (That word again, I thought. WTF?)

While we waited for ten minutes by the exterior lift for clearance to ride the lift up to the custody desk the detective remained motionless while I walked slowly in circles. He took the opportunity to ask a few questions – What was my job? Where did I live? – but I kept my answers short in case I was unknowingly breaking a law or it all became public 48 hours later as a result of a Press release or leak.

The green canvas bag full of language course books felt heavy on my back. I asked again how long my visit would last.

'Will it be over by 7.00 p.m.?'

It was unlikely, he said and asked why. I explained the Spanish class around the corner at 7.00 p.m.

If the interview would not be over by seven o'clock that meant a half-hour to book me in then an interview of an hour and a half? They had that much to say? The first interview only seemed to last 45 minutes.

As the minutes passed my body become a little more accustomed to the situation and the grip of shock and terror eased. I considered, then dismissed, the urge to make small talk. DC Woods obviously didn't feel the need either. I continued with my circle-walking in silence, bemused by the civility of it all. Here I was about to taken up as a 'prisoner' but I remained 'un-cuffed' and free to mill about. The detective presumably didn't feel threatened or thought I would do a runner, so, in some respects it was quite reassuring, even flattering.

Arriving at the custody desk I felt sick knowing that I was going to be rearrested and booked in. The custody officer worked our way through the same procedures – the basics (name, address details; reason for arrest) then the health and safety questionnaire (any illnesses, injuries). Are you taking medication? Yes, I replied, referring to the malaria pills ahead of the walking holiday. The custody officer asked for the type of malaria pill while reeling off the possible brands. I was intrigued. Were they experts?

Then the suicide question.

'Have you ever had suicidal thoughts?'

I didn't know how to answer this question but recalled Nightjack's advice.

'Are you having suicidal feelings now?'

I sighed and struggled for the first time. No-one had ever asked me that question, not so matter-of-factly and in a public area. How did one communicate feeling 'suicidal' to an absolute stranger in an unwelcoming environment anyway? When asked about one's psychological well-being, could the average Brit drop the ingrained, polite response 'Fine' and hurtle to the other end of the spectrum ('Um, I'm suicidal, thanks') in one fell swoop? For the thirty-nine years on the planet I had only ever been 'Fine, thanks'. It was a leap too far, but I needed to communicate the anger, anguish and frustration built up over 9.5 months. Especially when so much was at stake.

'A mixed bag,' I muttered, trying to be mature and non-whiny.

Whether the custody officer asked 'why?' I did not know, but I found myself explaining that I'd lost my film, my income and 'this' had been dragging on for nearly ten months.

'Nobody has told me anything,' I spat through a haze of anger, despair and disbelief, feeling my head was about to explode. So, in summary, given the tick-box options of the computer screen in front of him, I wanted to give him grounds to report my reply in the affirmative. After all, you could not take a person's 'life' and sanity away without there being a prospect of him or her feeling 'life-challenged'.

The officer didn't take the matter further. DC Woods, standing beside me, didn't flinch. They didn't care. Just another prisoner. Just another paedo. I had no idea what response was entered on my profile.

Next: the body-search and possessions check. I was asked to hand over my shoulder bag, remove my belt, my watch. I removed the bag from my shoulder, opened it up and removed an A5 pad and pen before handing over the bag.

'They have to be booked in too,' said DC Woods nodding at the paper and pen.

'I was going to take some notes.'

'You can't take anything into the interview.'

'Oh.'

'But you can ask your solicitor for paper and pen.'

Okay, I nodded, placing my notepad into the bag.

It was agreed the shoulder bag would be booked as one item whereupon Chris Woods placed it on the floor and rifled through its contents which included Spanish course books, my jumper, travel documents, my passport (which he made a point of checking) and my malaria medication. F*ck. Was this where my escape overseas (metaphorical, literal) to be thwarted? He rifled through it some more, but otherwise left it intact.

Moving round to the other desk I was asked to empty my pockets to allow them to scan me with a hand-held metal detector. My keys, wallet and other bits and bobs found themselves on the counter being logged on to the computer by the custody officer. From the pile of items he identified two USB memory sticks. One had been tucked into an inner trouser pocket, the other into my small leather case of keys. He held them up to DC Woods.

'Couple of USB memory sticks. What do you want to do with these?' he said looking straight at DC Woods with a nod and a wink (but without the wink).

Holy cow, I muttered in my head cursing myself for my ineptitude. Why hadn't I emptied my pockets of such things before I came? One memory stick contained a back-up of workplace documents, the other memory stick was a back-up of my own files (writing and editing documents). Neither USB stick was of any use whatsoever to the police, but they didn't know that and they no doubt would welcome a bit more material. What a day.

But to my surprise DC Woods, with a shake of the head, muttered a quiet 'No,' and waved them away. The two USB sticks joined the rest of my possessions to be collected on my departure.

Wow. I was quietly encouraged. Had I seen that correctly? The detective was unworried. It wasn't a problem. The police had the opportunity to confiscate a couple more memory sticks possibly full of juicy evidence, but, no, they were not interested. There was, I detected, a glimmer of surprise – an 'okay' – from the custody officer. That's a good sign, I thought, uncertainly to myself. It suggested that the investigating officer didn't think I was a walking, talking criminal. Maybe the interview was indeed a formality. They knew they hadn't found anything; there wasn't anything of use that would suggest I was a baddie. Or perhaps the wobbly state of mind had done its trick.

I was handed over to a young woman with 'Group 4 Security' badge sewn onto her jumper and escorted to a police cell. Private security firms working inside a police station. Interesting. As instructed, I removed my shoes and found myself in a cell once again. It wasn't such a shock, but my heart was sinking. They obviously wanted to talk about something. Informed that my solicitor was on his way, I sat and waited. It was bizarre to think I was getting used to the routine and the surroundings.

Fifteen minutes later DC Woods returned to say that my solicitor had arrived and I could speak to him before the interview. With my shoes back on I was escorted from my cell to a consultation room where my appointed solicitor, Alex, waited.

I took a seat and leant back on the wall in relative comfort as Alex explained that DC Woods wanted to speak to me about some deleted indecent images found on my computer. They were unofficially graded as being levels 1 to 4 (of 5 – level 5 being the most serious). What? I'm thinking. F*ck, no. I hadn't come across anything like that, surely, surely? My mind was suddenly racing. Alex gave nothing away. I limply protested my confusion, my innocence, feeling that the whole nightmare was wrapping itself around me like a black, heavy cloak. I was aware my words were weak which itself weakened me further. Holy f*ck, I could not believe it.

The day was now slipping into an abyss of the unexpected. I had my German friend in mind, but how could she have been involved in this? Struggling I repeated my previous assertions that I had seen normal stuff, but not what was being reported. Alex appeared grave and concerned; I was all a bit weak and nauseous. We were hardly a great team to be going into an interview. As an after-thought I asked if my imminent trip was threatened. Technically the police could prevent me from travelling, Alex replied, but he wouldn't expect it – I had turned up diligently to all my bail hearings, so I was not a flight risk.

While I sat there wide-eyed and shivering Alex talked through the interview options and recommended that I answered 'no comment' again during the interview.

'Let's see what they have,' he said. 'We can submit a statement later.'

As far as I am concerned, I was happy to mumble 'no comment' again until I knew what was going on. I recalled my words on the day of arrest that DC Hopkins had later spun into a capitalised admission presented formally on a piece of paper; an incident about which I was still smarting.

Alex was happy to comply with Chris Woods' suggestion that only the solicitor could provide a paper and a pen and handed the items over. We ran through a few other details regarding the interview including his belief that, in line with normal practice, only DC Chris Woods would be present, which was a relief. The fewer, the better.

Y1: 13. The Interview

The interview room was identical to (if not the same) as the room nine and a half months earlier, in fact more like a small, sound-proofed recording booth with a small table around which four people could squeeze. No cameras were visible. Clutching Alex's pad of paper and pen I was guided to my seat. A dual-tape recording deck sat on the table up against the wall. I sat facing the door with DC Woods sitting opposite me. Beside him sat DC Caine and beside me sat Alex Watt. Nobody knew me. They could all think I was guilty and were just following protocol.

Tapes were placed in the recorder and the introductions were made for the recording. I confirmed my name while DC Woods confirmed those others who were present in the room. And so, the questioning began.

DC Woods addressed me: 'Now you've been given disclosure prior to coming into interview in relation to indecent images found on a computer at your address. Is there anything that you'd like to comment on in relation to that?'

'No comment.'

'Now I understand that you're going to go 'no comment' for the rest of the interview which is obviously fine, it's your right, but we're still going to ask plenty of questions and I respect your right to answer no comment. What I'd ask is for you to respect me and let me finish my questions before you answer no comment. Is that fair?'

'No comment.'

I had in mind Nightjack's advice and solicitor Alison slamming the table nine months earlier berating me for replying 'yes' when asked by her if I wanted water in the pre-interview practice session. Nevertheless the transcript of the interview, received much later, noted: 'Officers comment that Mr Anderson had nodded his head whilst saying 'no comment' to the last question.'

DC Woods took the lead and started by asking the standard questions – similar to those asked during the first interview: who did the computer belong to; who used it; when used last? Who put it there? Passwords? Security? Had it been fixed in a shop? Had it had a virus? How long had I owned the computer? Software? Primary use of the computer? Discs? Memory sticks? Websites?

I was asked who had had access to the bedroom which struck me later as odd. The arrest had been prompted by 'intelligence' relating to events in 2007 (as DC Lauren Hopkins had mentioned in February) so how did they know it was in the bedroom at Meadow Road? I hadn't mentioned it. Or were they referring to Shrub Lane that apparently had not been part of the intelligence? Had the intelligence referred to a computer being in the bedroom at Meadow Road?

The talk turned to porn use: did I visit such sites? Which sites? Did the computer allow pop-ups? What did I do if there were pop-ups? Use of search engines? Was I sent images? What virus protection did I have? Did I have mass download software (whatever that was)?

No comment, no comment, no comment.

I was furiously writing down all the questions and anything else that popped into my head. I had not received the transcripts (or tapes) of the February interview and I was aware that I might not receive anything from this interview for months. I wanted to take away as much information as possible. A question might be asked or a detail revealed that might indicate the nature of the intelligence or other useful fact. I again wondered if they would ask about the use of a particular credit or debit card.

My rapid scribbling was not lost on the officers.

'Do you feel you have enough time to listen to questions … you're writing them down, so are you actually understanding what the question is? …. Because me personally, if I was writing down the questions I probably wouldn't be thinking about what the question was and what answer I wanted to give.'

'No comment.'

For the previous ten years I had not gone into any meeting without a pad and pen – it being my job to write up minutes of meetings.

DC Woods turned to another document saying it was a computer report. I was enjoying the experience less and less. He opened the report and explained its contents saying he had 22 sample images that he wanted to show me.

Across the table I saw that on the first page (of the A4 sheet) three images (large thumbnails) were evenly spaced down the page with a long line (of perhaps 50 to 100 characters) running horizontally across the page at the foot of each image. Each image was about the size of a matchbox. He spun the document around on the table surface allowing me to view the images and started talking about image number one. With my head spinning in this crazy, crazy situation and the small size of the image, it was a struggle to discern and assess the content of image 1 (which appeared to contain some human forms). Helpfully, DC Woods described the image and followed it up with questions. He described a naked, elderly gentleman with two young girls, also naked.

'Tell me about this image. Have you ever seen it before? Where did you get it from? Which site was it on? Was it sent to you?'

I was unable to process the image. It was too small for my spinning head as I continued to scribble notes. I desperately studied the long line of text to see if a date was contained therein or an email address or credit card number; a folder path, anything, but it all seemed computer gobbledygook, perhaps a computer reference number relating to the computer technician's report. Although I glanced at the second image of a girl sitting on a sofa (again too small to assess) my eye immediately fell on the (third) image closest to me across the table. As DC Woods described and asked questions about image 1 and 2, I scribbled down his questions while making an assessment of third image.

It was an image of a young black girl, under 10 years, standing smiling to camera with a T-shirt top on but nothing else.

'How much do you know about computers? Are you aware of what an unallocated cluster is?' I heard in the background as I scribbled, muttered 'no comment', scoured the line of text for clues and looked for clues of the image's origin.

Using my limited knowledge of photography and light, I suspected that the photograph was taken in Africa. For a moment I wondered whether the image belonged to a fundraising charity appeal. Although such campaigns often had images of youngsters in limited states of dress, my guess was immediately countered by the thought that it didn't really belong in such a context as it afforded the subject no privacy. It was a legitimate image of concern. One thing I knew without the merest shadow of a doubt was that I had not seen that image before, but I was determined to be open-minded. It could be a stray image from a charity site (but I doubted it), or it could have been attached to a junk email to myself or another computer user. Perhaps a stray image from some site somewhere. Whatever it was, the image was new to me.

'I can spell "unallocated cluster" if you'd like?' said DC Caine chipping in after which DC Woods explained the nature of unallocated clusters – deleted images that had left a slight trace on the computer.

Descriptions of the images and questions continued.

'Why are you looking at images like this? Did you agree the pictures were indecent? How did the image get on your computer? Did someone else use it? Is there any reasonable explanation for it being on this computer? Will you later claim it was part of some research?'

No comment; no comment; no comment.

DC Caine chipped in again: 'I don't want you looking at [these images] taking any pleasure out of them, so if we kind of [show] up one at a time'.

DC Woods complied with his colleague's request and used pieces of paper to reveal only one image at a time as they asked questions. I realised DC Caine was trying to rile me; there was some sort of good-cop, bad cop 'thing' going on. Although my head was still spinning, I was not fazed by his attempt to unsettle me. In fact I was becoming curious.

DC Woods turned the page to reveal three more images, each with a long line of characters. I again scoured the text line for some clue to its meaning, but nothing was obvious and I didn't have time to write it all down. As DC Woods described the image for the tape and asked questions, I muttered no comment, no comment and scribbled. The fourth image had underage boys engaged in a sex act with each other.

DC Woods: 'Did you view this on the computer? Which website did you log on to view this image?'

I knew absolutely unequivocally I had never seen the image or anything like it. Again, I forced myself to keep an open mind – email attachments; junk mail? After all, there were only 22 images? On a computer connected to the Internet for eight years?

More questions: 'Did you search for this? What website was it from? Were the pictures emailed to you? What did you do when you opened them?'

No comment; no comment; no comment.

'Did the pictures find their way onto the computer via a memory stick by mistake? Why did you look at it? Who sent it to you? Did you send it to others?'

Then more pictures – some solo images; others with interaction with adults. Each completely new to me. It was surreal; two worlds colliding. The adult world of sex and the world of youngsters. Bizarre. Image nine had a banner with a website name. Was this evidence of a website or just a logo on a particular image?

Questions: 'Why did you log on? Were you aware it included such images on it?'

I was becoming increasingly intrigued. This was not a matter of interpretation; it was the real McCoy, something certainly had been going on. Images 10, 11 and 12: posed images of youngsters. All completely new to me.

Suddenly there was a beeping from the tape machine; it was malfunctioning. The interview stopped and a new tape inserted. The sober 'interview vibe' was dropped as DC Woods fiddled with the machine. Credit to him, he maintained a serious, professional attitude, however, his colleague DC Caine discarded his 'interview-manner' and initiated jokey chat with my solicitor Alex who did not respond, sitting steadfast. I watched DC Caine making inappropriate wisecracks chummily slapping Alex on the arm in a 'we're old mates' way. Again Alex again did not respond. It was curious indeed. I had thought the interview and its circumstances deserved a bit more seriousness. DC Caine's interview manner had only been for the tape.

I was calm and curious as the interview re-started. I had been shown twelve images, another ten to go. As the taping re-started, Alex confirmed for the recording that there had been 'no conversations between the officers and Mr Anderson' while the tape-recorder had been switched off.

Image 13: a montage of two young females from a named website.

Questions: 'Have you visited this website before? What were you looking for? Was it a surprise? Did you ever visit a website with a similar address?'

No comment; no comment; no comment. Scribble; scribble; scribble.

More images: some solo, some with clear interaction with an adult. Unequivocally the real deal, but surreal. As each image was revealed I knew that I had never seen anything like this.

Questions: 'Why are you looking at this image? How does it make you feel now?'

Image 19: The matchbox size image was difficult to discern what was being displayed. A girl was engaged in a sexual act, but the upper half of the image was obscured by what appears to be a finger over the camera lens. But after a moment it became clear. It was not a finger covering the lens, but a blindfold on the girl. Totally bizarre and nothing I have ever seen before – of that there was total clarity. I was in a stunned state at the very existence of such images but, as far as I was concerned, I was now free from the investigation of wrongdoing. So whether it was junk emails, stray images that had somehow found their way onto the computer via memory sticks, viruses or websites, I didn't know.

'It's your opportunity to tell us about these images on your computer.'

'No comment.'

I was now lost to their world and on autopilot. When one is in a perpetual state of shock (as a lead player in a surreal situation) there is nowhere else to go. However, it was bizarrely now coupled with an increasing sense of relief.

'Can I ask what is so funny?' DC Caine asked.

'No comment.'

You seem to be smiling,' he said.

'No comment.'

'Do you find this funny – viewing these kinds of images?

I was shaken out of my musing by DC Caine's part-goading, part-observational comment.

I was unaware that I had been smiling (if indeed I had). I did not find it funny. In fact, I would argue I was not smiling as such, but I was certainly beginning to relax. I knew, as clear as a bell, the images had nothing whatsoever to do with me and I was learning something at last. In fact, to my mind, what I was being shown was Mannheim's handiwork. It had her fingerprints all over it. After nine and a half months, I now had an answer. And it felt good. At last, daylight.

'No comment.'

'Have you got any children?' asked DC Caine changing tack.

'No comment.'

'Young Nieces? Nephews?'

'No comment.'

'Do you work with children?'

No comment, but the point was made. Or was it in fact a threat? Were the police threatening trouble? Hassle? Had the officers done their homework? Did they know my family situation and intended to use them as a lever? What exactly was he implying?

If I had been smiling, I certainly wasn't now. Whether tactical or indicative of Caine's attitude, the veiled threat irritated and frustrated me.

'What was you initial reaction when you were arrested for this offence?' he continued.

'Were you kind of surprised? Did you scream your innocence from the rooftops?'

No comment; no comment; no comment, however, he should know I expressed bewilderment when the police visited, he had been there. How could I form an opinion when I had not been advised of the source, nature and detail of the only bit of information they had held – the infamous 'intelligence'?

Image 19 appeared to a homepage image of sorts for 'Crazy Paedo' with a montage of images. There was no ambiguity about its nature. I didn't know websites like that existed. It was as if Monty Python had done child porn. It was getting ridiculous. That said, it suggested the computer had in some way been in touch with websites.

DC Woods maintained a professional, subdued manner throughout as he asked his questions. I wondered what his views were? Did he have in his back-pocket statements from Mannheim and Linklee? Was he weighing up the evidence or validity of witness statements from the other housemates as he watched me? Having had my film work and files for nine months was he inclined to believe me rather than them? Was that why he had waved away the confiscation of the memory sticks at the custody desk an hour earlier? I was half-prepared for a question which began with the words 'Ms Mannheim has submitted a statement saying .....', but, no, nothing.

DC Caine continued his goading.

'Is that a website you visit regularly?'

'No comment.'

'Crazy Paedo. What does that mean?'

'No comment.'

'Are you a Crazy Paedo, Mr Anderson?'

'No comment.'

Image 20: another image of a home page of sorts for 'Paedo Paradise'. Again, another ridiculous image and title straight out of a Monty Python sketch.

'Tell me about this? How did it get there?'

No comment; no comment.

After a couple more images, the report was closed but not before a few follow up questions: 'What was your intention when looking at these images? For sexual gratification? Were you abused as a child which skewed your outlook on life? Do you have any questions for us? Have you had adequate time to listen to the questions? Is there anything you would like to clarify or add to the interview?'

DC Woods finally wrapped up.

'As I've explained ... should you go to Court, should these questions be put to you at Court and you come up with an answer, the Court will consider why you haven't mentioned it now. And the fact that you are not speaking to us now could go against you if you then come up with answers at Court. You understand that?'

'No comment.'

DC Caine soon followed up: 'These aren't the only images on your computer. There are a lot. Like a few thousand. This is just the provisional report.'

I didn't believe him. By this stage I had given up on Caine and didn't take anything he said seriously. He had had no notes in front of him during the previous hour and had spent half the interview leaning back in his chair with his arms folded firing out questions presumably in the hope of winding me up. He had no credibility in my eyes – just a teenage boy wanting to play cop.

The interview was concluded at 7.29 p.m. and the tape recorder was switched off and forms filled in. I was exhausted from all my scribbling, but I suspected there would be nothing in my notes of any use. Nothing I could investigate.

DC Caine's irreverent attitude returned: as the final details for the forms were read out including the citing of a code 'CTS81' (the importance of which I did not know), he turned to me and repeated sarcastically 'That's 'CTS81' if you want to write it down.'

It was a good thing the tape recorder had been turned off, because I suspected any courtroom would not be impressed by his tone or attitude – smug, complacent with a distinct lack of intellectual curiosity. Nevertheless, I dutifully scribbled it down as my opinion of some police officers plummeted and aware he was only able to speak in such a way because he carried a badge of state. That said, DC Woods was a model of professionalism.

'What are you going to do?' Alex asked DC Woods. It was clear Alex was seeking which course of action DC Woods intended to follow i.e. charge me or bail me. The detective appeared non-committal evading an answer. We rose to our feet and left the room. In contrast to my entrance, I was completely calm, as cool as a cucumber, with only one thing on my mind. Mannheim.

Y1: 14. Re-bailed

In the room that had hosted my pre-interview shock and wobble, I sat on the built-in bench seat waiting for Alex. The tension and swirling head was receding. I could breathe. After nearly ten months of anxiety I had finally been shown what the police had, and, as far as I was concerned, it had nothing to do with me.

Alex entered and sat down opposite me. He looked grave. He fixed his gaze on me and leaned forward.

'So, there we go. Do you have anything to say?' he asked in a noticeably challenging way. I realised that although he was on my side, he was coming at this from a point of total ignorance, but I was clear and sure in myself that the images had nothing to do with me. Relieved and exhausted, I relaxed against the wall.

'I haven't seen those pictures before,' I replied firmly meeting his eyes, but Alex didn't move his gaze away. He was looking for a glimmer of guilt, a shard of fear that I had been discovered. I was not sure if he believed me, but he should have noted that compared to my state an hour earlier I was now completely relaxed. If he didn't believe me, that was okay. That was a battle for another day.

'You look like the sort of person who keeps a diary. If we can show you were elsewhere, that would help.'

I shook my head. I had had a work desk diary but, having changed jobs, it would have been binned years ago. Shame, I had kept a diary from my teens until my early thirties, but events had overtaken my life and it was a habit I had dropped. Maybe I could have a look at my emails and piece something together, I thought.

'I'll see what I can do.'

So, what happens now? I asked. Alex advised me that there was the possibility that we submitted a statement of our own (as discussed before the interview), but he says he would consult with his colleague, Alison.

'She's very good,' he said.

He pointed at my eight pages of scribbles: 'The police were thinking about seizing your notes.'

Bizarre. Why would they do that? There was nothing of any use in them, certainly to the police. I had hoped the interview might reveal details of the investigation which I could investigate myself in my own time.

'Why? Can they do that?' I asked. 'What did you say?'

'I told them they were my notes and you were just holding on to them for me. If they ask, just say they're mine. Stick them in your pocket out of sight.'

Okay, I nodded, a bit disappointed that the officers would seek to scupper my day.

'I have to go now, I have another interview,' Alex said, rising to his feet.

'Okay, thanks. Thanks for your time.'

'Stay here and someone will collect you, take you to a cell and then re-bail you.'

And with that, Alex disappeared.

Shortly afterwards I was collected and escorted to the cell where I milled about for ten minutes thinking of my former co-tenants both now in Germany and wondering if they knew what was going on. Of course, they might not have had anything to do with it, but every fibre of my being was saying they were waist, nay, neck deep.

DC Woods collected me from the cell and walked me back to the custody desk. Was he questioning why I wasn't rattled? Did this confuse him? He seemed disappointed, quiet. I guessed that he felt progress hadn't been made and it meant more work for him.

My belongings were returned in exchange for a signature. I signed a re-bail sheet confirming receipt. I was required to answer bail at 10.00 a.m. on Wednesday 20 January. Foolishly, unlike my previous re-bailing hearings earlier in the year, I hadn't brought a calendar printout to compare it with other events that day, but from memory it looked pretty good, but I noted that I would have to book a whole day off work. Now that things were moving, it would be a long day.

Packed up and ready to go, DC Woods escorted me through a security door and down several flights of stairs. All in total silence. Still appearing disappointed, he opened the door leading onto the street and stood to the side letting me pass. 'Lovely,' I heard myself utter in a rather upbeat, unruffled fashion before slipping out into the night.

Wow, life, the weirdness of it all, but it felt good. It was approaching eight o'clock, my Spanish language class would be in their break and I could slide in for the second half of the class. I felt I ought to go, but the class would be revisiting the work conducted in the first half of the lesson. My late arrival would make me look like a slacker. Switching on my mobile telephone I picked up a voicemail message from my father three hours earlier asking for news left shortly after 5.00 p.m. (a time when I was being booked in to custody and a whole different world).

I dialled and spoke to my mother.

'How was it?' she asked.

'Good news and bad news,' I replied in a relaxed, upbeat fashion. 'They did find some stuff, but it has nothing to do with me.'

In normal circumstances a person could have reflected upon (and been angry for) those youngsters caught up in the abuse, but the photographs were competing against the emotional and psychological exhaustion from the day's events, the stress of 294 days on bail, not to mention the shock and, bizarrely, relief on learning of Mannheim's involvement. So, with life on bail numbing me to the trials and tribulations of others, I cycled home and explained to my parents that there was arguably a case to answer, but it was not my case. It was someone else's.

Y1: 15. Nepal

[Reader, this is the first (of three) chapters mentioned in the Foreword, you can skip it if it pleases. A holiday break.]

After a few more days in the office, I jumped on a plane and headed to Nepal. I arrived in Kathmandu and met the rest of the tour group and our guide, Hirum, over the next fourteen hours. The group largely consisted of Australians, New Zealanders and Canadians. Smiles and cheerfulness are easily feigned if everything smells and sounds different.

A few late-night coffees while chatting to a new Australian friend (coupled with a busy head reliving the police interview) meant I did not sleep. In fact I spent the first night adjusting to the new timezone and old thoughts of a criminal investigation thousands of miles away. I feared that my two weeks away would not be the escape I was hoping for. The first morning started with a briefing and then a walking tour of Kathmandu which included visits to the Bodhnath Stupa and the Hindu temple Pashupatinath and, after watching open-air funeral pyres on the banks of the river, the temples and tourist areas in and around Thamel.

The following morning a rickety old bus carried us along mountain and valley roads for six hours to Pokhara, a town used as a base for hikers visiting the Annapurna region. An afternoon of exploring the towns and shops, wandering around the edge of lake, reading and drinking coffee in local establishments began to establish a slower pace to my churnings within. The following day we drove to village of Naya Phul, disembarked and began our walk in the Annapurna lowlands – firstly along dirt-tracks in the valley floor and then up stone staircases built into the valley sides along the Modi Khola River through the villages of Birethanti and Kimche. We soon had the Annapurna peaks in our sights including the recognisable fishtail peak Machhapuchhare and reach our night-time lodge in the village of Ghandruk.

Our hike the following morning was to the village of Landruk across the valley. It was the first whole day of hiking involving a steep descent into the valley swamped in the warmth of the sun and a relatively steep climb up to Landruk for lunch. In preparation for the trip I had endeavoured to do a bit of fitness training fearful of my knees, lungs and limbs, but I was fine and was soon happily zooming up valley sides aware I was simultaneously burning through some of the toxicity that had built up inside me during the previous nine months. If I wasn't zooming, I was zoning out as I meandered along ridges and up and down slight inclines. The climate was perfectly temperate – in the sun it was warm and one could work up a sweat, but in the shade of the valley or tree canopy, it could get chilly. From Landruk we descended slowly to the village of Tolka for the night.

The following day we hiked to a pass at Bhichok Deorali and had lunch at Pothana, all the while taking in the sights of the Annapurna range. The conversations with co-travellers were all perfectly pleasant; my Australian friend was a police officer (or rather a civilian with police affiliation) who had been investigating a corrupt police officer. The investigation had produced much incriminating evidence, but apparently the matter was being dropped by his superiors for various reasons much to his frustration whereupon he shared his overall cautious attitude towards police personnel. I said nothing of my own predicament, but it was good to know that the competency and integrity of the police was not taken for granted in other parts of the world. After all, it was a profession like any other, not a vocation for the righteous.

I took photos of the mountain ranges pleased to be able to capture images I could use for screensavers if and when my computer was returned. I wouldn't have to rely on stock images of misty mountains, I had my own and they would remind me of a real (rather than imagined) world beyond my walls. For all my efforts I could never shake the trouble back in the UK, but a heavy heart was easier to carry at altitude. After much walking we eventually headed down through the village of Dhampus into the Yamdi Khola river valley to Phedi from where we made a short return journey to Pokhara.

The following day we left for white-water rafting on the Seti river. After a very early start and lots of sitting around we descended to the river and lashed ourselves to something seemingly built by contestants on the Krypton Factor. I was in Nepal for the mountains, so I was pleased when the morning and half-afternoon of rafting concluded and we drifted up to a shallow beach of shingle surrounded by massive valleys of lush greenery. A late afternoon was spent lazing in hammocks in the camp by the beach and a night in wood cabins. I'm sure the place had a name, but it is lost somewhere in the forest. Whatever its name, it was one of those places where you both lose and find yourself. A place of rest.

The following morning we boarded the rafts again for a few hours and disembarked at Gai Ghat. A bus delivered us to Chitwan National Park for a pleasant stay in a lodge. A jeep excursion through the thick forest skirting misty swamps felt like a trip into Jurassic Park. The travel guide proudly stated:

'Tiger sightings are very rare these days; however, luck may be on our side!', but my concerns were about the velociraptors. A mid-sized dinosaur disguised as a rhinoceros was spotted too close for my liking, but was too lazy to charge the jeep. For all its excitement, I did pick up a few more screensavers before we arrived back at the lodge for an elephant trek.

The trip came to an end the following day and the group split up; some travellers headed north back to Kathmandu, others south to India. I spent my last few days in Kathmandu on trips to the old city of Bhaktapur, an Everest-sightseeing flight and clothes and picture shopping. A flight back to London landed me back in my sea of troubles.

Year Two (Y2)

Y2: 1. Preview

I braced myself for a difficult year. I had spent New Year's day with my sister's family in Shropshire. She and her husband (along with my three other siblings) remained oblivious to my criminal status, but after the interview and events of early December I could only assume police matters would shortly take a turn for the worse. Perhaps family and others would know soon. Perhaps that New Year would be the last time I would see them before lives and relationships changed forever.

In early January the UK was hit by the worst snow for years. The country ground to a halt for a significant part of January. There was limited public transport, commuters couldn't commute and all seemed right with the world. On a daily basis Oxford emptied early, leaving the town calm, quiet and white. It was also the season when James Cameron's 3D movie *Avatar* was released. I had missed the crowds of December and watched in a relatively empty cinema on the first day of the snow. The film's blue, 3D idealised world transported me to a world far away from the previous eleven months. What people did before cinema to escape turmoil, I do not know.

I recalled Alex's question to DC Woods at the end of the December interview about what the detective intended to do. There was uncertainty suggesting I might well be charged on the spot. Any sense of doom was countered-balanced by DC Woods not confiscating the two memory sticks and (what I detected as) his further uncertainty during the interview. Was the detective weighing up the other housemates? How much did he know of them? It would make little difference, because, if questioned, Mannheim would certainly pin everything on me and profess total ignorance. Had DC Woods been expecting me to land Mannheim in it?

At the beginning of each year I usually wrote a preview of the year to come. My preview of the previous year (written six weeks before my arrest) had been a wish-list based around updating the film, networking and developing projects while establishing an income from video editing. But twelve months later my 'preview of the year ahead' was wholly focussed on the fall-out from the rubbish I had found myself in. These troubles (or, in code, my 'Pickle') would affect my living arrangements, my work arrangements (current) and career plans (what was left of them) and any leisure activities. In fact there was not one area of my life that it would not touch.

My preview for the 12 months ahead were:

Living Arrangements. Would I move into my own place? I had some funds from a modest inheritance from a family friend and had thought of using it as a deposit on a flat or house. My preview noted that if I did not find myself in my own property by the end of the year, it would be because I was safely accommodated in a prison cell. That said, I decided to be positive and proactive and made a start of looking at houses not knowing how the timeframes of pending legalities would complicate matters (or not).

Employment. The options were similarly stark: I would either remain in my administration job or I would be fired (unless I resigned first). Then, having spent a year or so staring at prison walls, I would be relatively unemployable.

Career plans (film). Progress: none – the film was in a police lock-up. I considered the possibility of writing screenplays, but nothing kills the creative spark like being on police bail for a sexual offence.

Leisure and distractions. Nepal had been a much-needed tonic. Perhaps I could slip in a bit of travel. Watching DVDs were a shoo-in for predictions for the year. Exercise in the form of squash, martial arts and running would also continue.

Everything depended on a handful of people sitting in the police station a few miles away. In summary, I wrote off the whole year. Even if matters were brought to a conclusion in the spring, a recovery would not be managed before December. It would be a wholly unproductive 12 months. A year to be endured.

Y2: 2. Legal Preparation

I compiled a statement for Alex and the solicitors in response to the police interview and emailed it to Alex a week ahead of the scheduled interview on 20 January. In the covering email I explained that in the twelve months leading up to the alleged offence I had approached the police three times (once in person, twice on the phone) over my concerns about my escalating difficulties with housemates and that I might be on the receiving end of serious 'unpleasantness' from my co-tenants:

> *I spoke to a sympathetic [police] woman who gave advice ... I wrote down a code/reference number at the time, but I believe I threw it away when I was clearing up some months later and/or when I moved house. However, I believe it was (or had something to do with) 'white' and/or a colour. Perhaps a PC White? Did such an individual operate the phones [at the time]?*

I started the document itself with a clear statement:

Further to the [interview in December], I can
confirm that I didn't recognise any of those
images. I sincerely believe I would have
remembered those images if I had come across
them. The computer was in a shared house for
eight years and accessed by housemates and
houseguests. It was not password-protected.

I explained my fears had stemmed from the housemate's erratic behaviour, rent problems and his aggressive girlfriend who, I believed, was engaged in benefit fraud – something I had declined to assist them with (and eventually thwarted). I had sought advice from the landlord and the police, having witnessed her use the legal system to intimidate and harass others. I referred to the existence of a video diary (explaining the living arrangements and recording my fears) compiled for a third party in the event that she initiated legal proceedings or made allegations. In the video I even had footage of the computer equipment set up as an editing suite in my bedroom in the property.

During the tenancy with the housemates I had had visions of Mannheim storming into my room and contriving a 'flare-up' by disrupting or trashing my computer and hard-drives knowing it might be the one thing (my precious film) that would 'set me off'. I was afraid I might indeed react (at the very least physically restrain her). After a 'struggle' she would call the police and claim I had assaulted her. My hope was that a video diary (and having the police on speed-dial) would help me manage the situation. That said, I did not refer to such scenarios, I kept the document to one page and as factual as possible.

I did refer to the computer dialogue boxes: '[I] recall two occasions (before I left Meadow Road) when my computer threw up a message / dialogue box stating that someone was trying to gain control of my computer' as it would be something I would refer to at a later date (in any defence setting and certainly in court).

Hopefully the document summarised my position for Alex and his colleagues. I didn't want to find myself in a situation where Alex or Alison said 'Why didn't you tell us this before?' I wanted them to be clear of my opinion that it was possible that these two individuals may be involved in this matter to cause me maximum inconvenience and trouble.

I gave Alex a few days to digest the email and document with the full intention that we should speak before the interview on 20 January. I had questions: Would the document in full be forwarded to the police? Or would just a few paragraphs (or sentences) summarising my position be forwarded for consideration? Would it be advantageous to submit it ahead of the interview (to demonstrate my cooperation) or during an interview itself? Or even afterwards?

So it was that on one lunch-break I summoned up the courage to call Alex to talk criminal law. I could never make such calls from my office building. Therefore, shivering on a nearby street, with the cold wind blowing in my ears, I phoned. My feeling after the December interview had been that he was unsure what to think of me, but reaching him that cold January day I detected no judgement. He confirmed that he had indeed received my statement and that he would consult with colleagues on ways forward. The plan, as it stood, was not to forward the one-page statement to the police but to wait until the interview and see what happened.

I asked whether he thought the 20 January interview would take place; the police had not been ready to move forward in December and the extended Christmas break (and January snow which had shut down much of the country) might have delayed developments. Alex couldn't say. I also explained that I was thinking of buying a house but a criminal charge (and/or the loss of my job) could prove problematic at which point Alex volunteered that he could not be sure whether 'it would be a custodial sentence'.

WTF? Who was talking about prison time?

Perhaps he had indeed reached a judgement. I was only talking about a criminal charge followed possibly by a trial. Who said anything about a guilty verdict? My question had arisen as a result of the cost of defence and paying a mortgage having lost an income.

'Treat it like an asset,' he said unaware of the effect his words had upon me.

Meanwhile, I continued to keep an eye on the national press for stories about police performance and court cases. One such story focused on the case of a woman (Susan May) who had been jailed for 10 to 12 years for murdering her aunt. She was adamant that she was innocent and, as her supporters reported, had only been imprisoned as a result of a biased and inefficient police investigation. Elements of her case sounded horribly familiar. Phrases had been taken out of context and the police had adopted the view early on that she had been responsible and built a case against her accordingly. Her supporters pointed to examples of the police either ignoring evidence or being selective in the presentation of evidence and the lines of investigation followed. So, on reflection, I remained wary of what information should be passed to the police. I was happy to follow the solicitors' guidance ahead of the interview a few weeks later on 20 January. And with that I returned to considering life-options for the rest of the year.

Y2: 3. Review

Approximately eleven months later at midnight I checked my phone. No message. No news. I watched as the phone's display changed to Wednesday 8 December: one year had passed since the fifty-minute interview with the police .... after which nothing had happened. I had been re-bailed a further six times during the year (on 20 January, twice in March, July, October and November).

In fact, in December my bail status had technically lapsed. I had received no formal notice of bail extension since being informed by phone that I was being re-bailed for the eleventh time in November. Was that legal? Did that mean anything? In a sense I was free from the State for the first time in over 650 days? Aware of the anniversary (and nearly two months short of two years since the police visit), my mother suggested I should call the police and find out what was going on. No, I said. Just leave it. I didn't have the strength, besides, in my head I thought that perhaps it would all go away. No need to stir it up. Let it play out.

A few days later I learnt the truth: Wednesday 2 February – the day on which I was next to answer bail. A date two weeks short of two years on police bail. In the meantime I would have to fake a second Christmas of jollity. I had received an invitation to spend a few days at Christmas at my brother Antony's new home in Lincolnshire. As grateful as I was for the invitation, I was not sure I could sit comfortably as we reflected on events in the previous twelve months and what might lie in store for us in the following twelve months. Sitting next to a roaring fire sipping wine I would be asked how I was and why I had not been seen for a while and: Why did I look tense? Why hadn't I been myself recently? Was it the job?

Caught at the wrong time, my composure might wobble. More stress. More indignity. Besides, I might receive a call from DC Woods and find myself called in for a final meeting before Christmas. So, after consideration, I thought I would politely decline and write off Christmas as a low-key few days.

The stress had been telling and it manifested as an impatience with everything, even taking the phone call from my father that I was about to enter my third calendar year of being on bail with still with no idea as to the police's reasoning (more particularly the intelligence that had triggered their visit).

'This is Home calling,' my father had chirped down the telephone. 'Just to let you know that there is a brown envelope here addressed to you. What you want us to do with it?'

The message was a few hours old. I phoned my parents straightaway and reached my father. I got straight to the point. No time for pleasantries.

'Yes, well, can you open it?' I asked, vexed. I was not sure I could pace around my own house for 24 hours with it on my mind before being able to pick it up from them in person.

'Okay, I need to put down the phone,' he said not aware the effect the delay had on me. It went quiet. I only heard some paper rustling. Then the phone went dead.

F*ck. Tit. The old man. He had probably fumbled the phone when picking up the handset again. I immediately phoned the number to be met by an engaged tone and message: 'The phone is in use,' the BT Home messaging service announced. 'Please leave a message.'

This set the pattern for the next seven minutes. I waited. I phoned. It was always engaged. I phoned, then waited. The phone finally rang. It was my mother. She started reading from the beginning of the re-bail notice – 'Further to the interview on 8 December .....'

Oh for f*ck's sake. The old woman. Knowing the format of these bail notices like the back of my hand, I was fully aware that the important information was at the end of the notice. To read the whole re-bail notice would take 45 seconds at her PD James reading rate. I didn't have 45 seconds. This was the rest of my life we were talking about.

'You want to skip to the end?' I muttered, calmly. 'The date.'

'What's the date?'

F*%k$@(Fu!k£.

Then 'ums' and 'ers'.

'2 February.'

'What?!'

'2 February.'

'How can that be?' I asked in exasperation.

The frustration was in fact mixed with a certain amount of relief that the notice was not calling me into the police station within the next 96 hours, or the next 10 days. No, it was 51 days later. And 15 days short of the second anniversary of my arrest. How could that be?

I rambled on for a few minutes in the same exasperated vein. How could I defend myself? How could I find witnesses to support me? Peoples' memories fade. They (and I) lose things ('evidence') that could be tied to a date – work diaries, restaurant bills, cashpoint receipts, even phone records. I thought of my enquiry to the mobile phone provider over a year earlier regarding calls made during my tenancy in Meadow Road – the company couldn't guarantee records had been kept.

As for my preview for the year, it had been wholly off-target. I realised I would have to write another preview in a few weeks' time at the end of a year but not before I had written a review of the year gone by.

Y2: 4. Work

The review. I had remained in administrative post. I would slip out of the office for the bail hearings only to return an hour later having been re-bailed and without any colleague being the wiser. On one level I had not really minded being stuck in the administrative job. After all, there was an income, but I was aware I could lose it in a flash, so there was no reason to seek alternative employment. (A couple of work colleagues had left and not been replaced, so I was kept busy.) As my workload grew I was too tired in the evenings to push the writing forward. I tried planning my creative work (as a form of motivation) and monitoring my progress in my diary (as another form of motivation). This was done by writing a 'weekly Preview', after which I wrote a 'Review' of the week. After a while the Previews began to read like a Review:

Entry week beginning 20 September:

> *Preview: A dull tedious week. Busy at work. Tired and no time for writing and editing. A complete waste of time and energy.*
> *Review: Correct. As above.*

Entry week beginning 27 September:

> *Preview: Another totally f'king waste of my life. Frustration and wholesale lack of creativity. No writing, editing.*
> *Review: Correct.*

Occasionally I would get a shock to my working day. One non-descript weekday afternoon the phone rang while I was in an informal meeting with a colleague. The call was from the receptionist three floors below.

'David, I have the Thames Valley Police wanting to talk to you.'

What? F*ck, holy f*ck. Where did that come from?

My heart, lungs, kidneys, liver, stomach and bowels spontaneously turned into heavy metal and plummeted south, crushing any illusion of relative peace and sanity. I quickly re-checked the receptionist's spoken words and registered the words 'on the line'. It would seem, the police were not present in the building itself, but I could not bank on anything. Though blind-sided by the horror that my misery had finally found its way to my workplace, I responded conscious that a colleague was sitting three feet away from me. 'Okay, put them through.'

'Hello,' I said, 'I'm David Anderson.' (Why did they ask for me, I think? Or did they ask for me by name, I think? Did they know me?)

'Hello, I'm Sargeant Stevens from Thames Valley Police and we're investigating a crime by a possible student of yours.'

He's innocent, stop bothering him, I instinctively thought while experiencing some relief that I didn't appear to be the reason for the call, nevertheless, I wondered whether the police officer knew to whom he was speaking. I didn't recognise his name, but did he know mine? I was known to more officers in his police station than I knew, but there was no indication in his voice or manner that suggested he knew my identity. The officer described the person-of-interest, but it wasn't anybody known to my department. The conversation wrapped up, I replaced the receiver with a sigh of relief but it was a sudden reminder in the middle of a relatively quiet bail-period how my troubles could rear its head in the workplace.

Other reminders were more mundane. My computer calendar at work was set to 'month-view' (whereupon I might switch to 'week-view' to conduct my business for the week). At the end of July I had added the entry '10.00 a.m. Chris & Alex' (i.e. police detective and duty solicitor) to the calendar for the answering of bail on 20 October. At the time the October calendar 'event' was three mouse-clicks away: one click to August view, a second click to view September and a third click to view October where the 'Chris and Alex' entry sat half-way down the screen. So, the re-bail date was well beyond the calendar's 'event-horizon'. But the days passed and as I logged on to my computer in the bright mornings, the calendar event entry soon became two clicks away (but beyond the event-horizon). Then it was one click away. Then suddenly it was no clicks away and I would log on to find the calendar-entry blinking at me half-way down the screen – twenty squares into the month.

I could save myself some discomfort by clicking week-view and it would disappear. Days passed and the twenty squares would be faded out and the event shone ever more brightly. The event slowly moved along the row one day at a time before jumping up to the next row until no amount of clicking could remove it from view. The event's arrival soon qualified for being described as double-figure hours away. I braced myself for the moment when I would find myself separated from the event by a slim purple line. There were calendar entries that followed the 'Alex & Chris' entry but I didn't see them; their very existence threatened by the 'events' of the 20 October, a date marked only by the calendar entry of two innocuous names.

Y2: 5. House

Living arrangements. I had moved into my own place during the year taking Alex's advice and treating the house as an asset. I had wondered whether the timing of the purchase was irresponsible. Would I have to sell it immediately? Would someone have to sell it for me?

The purchase had been a close-run thing. The offer had been accepted and the vendor had been keen to hurry it along. We were soon to reach a point when everything had to be finalised – the completion date had been set for 9 April, ten days after the re-bail date (and inevitable charge, I had thought at the time). Money transfers had been scheduled to start in late-March. I asked my solicitor when was the very latest things could change. The question was framed around the possibility of a vendor's decision to pull out of the sale, but I was really trying to establish the latest time I could withdraw. I was told it would be 5.00 p.m. on the Tuesday 30 March – coincidentally both the day and time of the (then) next scheduled police interview.

I had been at a loss and pondered the options and whether it would go up to the wire. Could I arrive at the police station earlier and see if there was an envelope waiting for me or establish if the interview would take place? Or even if a charge would be forthcoming? What if the interview ran on and I was unable to communicate a decision on the house and transfer of funds? Despite the dilemma I had been feeling a bit better since the previous re-bailing on 2 March. I could not quite explain it. Perhaps it was hormonal. I wondered if it was the imminent arrival of British Summer Time when the long, sunny days chased the darkness back into the depths of the police station.

I kept alert for other signs, particularly in the week preceding 30 March. At the beginning of the month a mystically, cool, calm, Bangladeshi friend (without any prompting) suggested March would be a good month for me. My martial arts sensei noted that the Chancellor's dropping of Stamp Duty that week (the end of March) was a good sign for the purchase of the house. Even my horoscopes were alluding to positive energy. But I had also noted that 30 March fell in Week 13 of the year. Lucky 13.

At lunchtime before the day of reckoning (ten working hours before I was scheduled to appear at the police station), I received a message that an envelope was waiting for me at my parents' home. I turned over all the possibilities in my head. Why post the letter? They had never posted a re-bail notice to me before. Why this time...? It could of course be junk mail – a mail-shot from an estates agent. Arriving at their home I found my parents anxiously waiting in the kitchen. My mother handed me the brown A5 envelope. To the observer I might have appeared relaxed, in fact I was just glazed, resigned and nauseous, exhausted by hours of deliberation. The letter did indeed have a postmark suggesting it came from the police and it did look like something the police would send. I opened it. Indeed it was a re-bail notice:

I immediately scanned down to the last words on the bail sheet where I knew I would find the re-bail date. I stared at it and felt my face contort in a 'What the ....?!' expression. I stared at it for a moment longer to be sure that I was not mis-reading it.

'I'm re-bailed to the 27 July.' I did a quick calculation in my head. 'That's three and a half, no, four months away!'

The slop of mixed feelings landed on my head. There was the tremendous relief that I would wake the following morning in the certain knowledge that I wouldn't be facing the detectives across the table before the day had ended. But four months! I had never been re-bailed for such a long period after the first bailing. I took it as an unequivocal sign to go ahead with the purchase of the house. As the evening wore on I relaxed, breathed and pondered the reasons behind the extended delay, concluding that the police must have been cooling to the idea of me as a baddie. Perhaps they had had a breakthrough in the investigation of the others in the house Mannheim and Linklee (arising from my parents' comments to DC Hopkins on the day of arrest and review of the electoral roll among other sources). Perhaps complications arising from dealing with agencies in another jurisdiction (Germany) were responsible for the delays.

'Why don't you challenge it?' my mother had asked.

I understood her point, but I didn't have the energy. I would rather savour the relief. Besides I was not inclined to rock the boat, it might sail away, or even sink. At least I had four months of relative peace and I could move into an 'asset'.

Y2: 6. Health and Signs

One matter I had not addressed in my original Preview of the year was health, but by the end of the year I reflected that the twelve months had largely been about managing my 'head', my psychology. Simmering anxiety is as much physical as it is psychological.

There were no legal developments to react to, so the challenge during the year was trying to keep level-headed. I welcomed little reminders to keep my troubles in perspective, to see the Pickle as part of a journey; one such reminder was found in the Pixar movie *Cars* and articulated in Brad Paisley's lyrics of the closing credits track, 'Find Yourself':

> *We go through life*
> *So sure of where we're headin'*
> *And then we wind up lost*
> *And it's the best thing that could have happened*
> *'Cause sometimes when you lose your way*
> *It's really just as well*
> *Because you find yourself*
> *Yeah, that's when you find yourself*

I was also alert to nods of encouragement. I concluded that the cosmos talks to its children. And it talks through 'signs' that have been read and understood (and misunderstood) through the ages. In the absence of news from the police as to the direction of my case (or rather, my life) the cosmos stepped in with clues from birds (emptying their bowels on me – August) to the surprise repair of damaged roads.

Commuting from my new house in Wantage (a half-hour drive) meant that I soon became very familiar with the roads. I would find myself swinging the car around the same old pot-holes, bumps and cracks in the road, each hammering my peace of mind. Life on bail made real; like the *Cars* movie storyline the broken tarmac was a manifestation of the life journey I was travelling – everything was disintegrating. But in late-summer, having sought distraction in an evening of sports, I found that a pothole around which I had been manoeuvring my car for years had suddenly disappeared. It had gone. The tarmac was smooth, soft, pure. It was a reminder that things could be mended, are mended. I should have patience. No sooner had the thought occurred to me and I was considering its implications (and questioning my sanity, after all it was one pot-hole of many) I found myself needlessly guiding the car first to the left on a bend and then to the right because two long-standing potholes too had gone. Just disappeared. Everything was smooth. Life was good. Maybe things were indeed on the mend.

I was also reminded of the purchase of the house earlier in the year when I had pressed for a sign on whether I should proceed knowing that the date of the interview coincided to the minute with the last moment I could withdraw from the house purchase. I was rewarded with a re-bailing notice twenty-four hours before the deadline bailing me for a further four months.

On holiday in Asia a year before my arrest I had visited a Pagoda near Bangkok and made an offering; in return I was given a scroll on which my fortune had been written. One of the last lines printed on a scroll read: 'Beaming Victory is answered in legal dispute'. I dismissed it at the time, after all there was no prospect of me being involved in a legal dispute, was there? On the same trip a fortune-teller reported, after a face-and-hand reading, that I was going to have a good life, move house et cetera, but he ended with a note of warning and a note of encouragement. The warning: be advised, someone was cheating me, therefore be careful; the encouragement: 'Mr David has good sixth sense'. Furthermore, black cats were often found loitering in my path and always at a time when bail was being extended, but they were often undecided about their movements, not all crossed my path. Luck was not always on my side, apparently.

My psychology of my Pickle was made manifest in pretty much everything – from the fate of trapped butterflies to the cleanliness of kitchen pans.

The butterfly: One Saturday morning, as I was dozing in the warmth and comfort of my bed, I saw a butterfly struggling on the inside of the window. I lay there wholly identifying with the creature trapped in a hostile environment unable to escape into a beautiful world beyond. Having bonded with the butterfly my conscience got the better of me and, with the aid of an upturned mug, I caught the creature and manoeuvred it out of the window. It flew to its freedom only to be caught and trapped in a cobweb, beyond my reach.

The pan: Forty-eight hours before answering bail at the police station for a ninth time I endeavoured to finish the contents of my fridge and had some scrambled eggs late at night. The frying pan, being a traditional 'stick pan' (as opposed to being 'non-stick') proved difficult to clean so I decided to let it soak overnight. I realised that I wouldn't have time to wash it up the following morning, so it dawned on me that the next time I would see it I would most probably hold a different legal status. I imagined myself later that week standing at the sink slowly and dejectedly scrubbing the non-non-stick-pan soiled in an earlier age of innocence as I waited for the local newspaper to print 'In Court News'. But rinsing a mug in the morning before dashing out the door, I saw the pan soaking in the sink. It occurred to me that I did in fact have time to wash it up, but then I noted that if I did clean the pan, it would interfere with the image of me standing at the sink later that week. But then, fuck it, I thought, why shouldn't I throw caution to the wind, be proactive and impose my will on events? I grabbed a sponge and attacked the pan to break the cycle and throw unpredictability into the mix. At least I tried. The egg's remains held fast. So I left it, knowing it would be scrubbed clean by a man awaiting a Crown Court trial.

Returning to the house a few days later I spotted the pan and its leading role in the turmoil of my imaginings forty-eight hours earlier. It had all come to nothing, but my whole being had been through the mill. I wondered what damage was being done to my body as it dealt with the downs and (sudden) ups of life on bail. I knew it would not be long before the edginess returned and the requirement to maintain the composure for the outside world. Was there a word that accurately described 'composure masking turmoil'? A word that captured the tension between the two extremes: the layer of composure exhibited and the stunned, viscous nausea within?

As the months went on I wondered what kind of 'fight' I had in me, not only the fight in a court of law but also the energy to endure its repercussions – the wholesale reorganisation of one's life and expectations. When feeling weak, uncertain and doubtful about my own strength I reflected on two episodes that helped restore my resolve. The first episode was my memory of standing at the corner of my bed during the (troubled) tenancy doubting my sanity over whether to video record evidence of the deteriorating relationship (with Mannheim and Linklee) in case 'there were difficulties' at a later date. At the time I was suddenly visited by feelings of both reassurance and encouragement to proceed with video recording because (as the sensation suggested) I did not know how useful the recordings might prove to be at a later date. The second episode that served to restore my resolve was the response of my mind, body and soul to the recovered images shown to me in the police interview twelve months earlier. I had exited that room cool, calm and collected. During all the turmoil endured since the arrest, it had been the one moment when I was at my most serene. I walked out of that room a 'free man'. So, in the difficult moments I always referred back to that beacon of clarity or 'golden nugget' as I called it. When I was in any doubt I endeavoured to revisit the instinctive reaction to the images.

That said, there were some dark times, difficult times. I got angry, got frustrated, got mad at the madness itself. One deep frustration was the echo of the smug taunts of DC Caine in the police interview particularly when I was being kept in the dark about the investigation's nature and origins. A year into the bail period there was a vexing time as I despaired at the possible continuation of such tactics. I imagined being on the witness stand in the Crown Court still blinking in ignorance of the intelligence that had brought the police to my door and the selectiveness and twisting of the information brought to the court by the police.

The news media was running stories of people caught up in similar difficulties. One such story related how the police had received intelligence about illegal computer porn only to come to the conclusion later that it had been placed on the device by the suspect's work colleague. Another article told the story of a grandfather who had committed suicide after police visited and seized his computer because an overseas agency had registered his computer for downloading one indecent image. Even the *Daily Mail* newspaper had been sympathetic to him.

I was conscious of my own mental well-being. As the frustration and anger bedded in and helpless to influence events, my mind turned to one outcome that would shut DC Caine up. One of the houses I had viewed before settling on the Wantage property had been a farmhouse beside a railway line with trains speeding past. I had never been near a train going at such speed. The property itself was accessed by a rail crossing situated at the end of the garden. And so it was that frustration with the delays and the police's withholding of information (the 'intelligence') that led me to think of speeding trains at Appleford. A few well-timed steps on to a train track would wake DC Caine and the rest of them up. For me it would be quick and I would be conscious to the end. It would be an unequivocal statement all of my own. I would take back control. However, it would not be done before I had prepared media packs for the national Press of (the then) thirteen months of delays and put the police in the spotlight. Perhaps the newspapers stories would wipe the smug smiles off the faces of the likes of Detective Caine. Who knew, perhaps the Press (or even YouTubers) could even put the police to shame and move the investigation along to a satisfactory conclusion. I suppose others in a similar position to me act out of a sense of shame, others out of despair, others out of fear of embarrassment, but for me it would be out of protest. A wail of frustration. But the dark times passed to become overcast times, but having lived through that period I was never judgemental when I read in the papers that others had succumbed to taking matters into their own hands. That said, there was one other thing that was certainly holding me back: if I did follow through there was the danger that Mannheim would 'get away with it' and that was something I could not accept. Much later I came across a reference to a Japanese proverb that said something along the lines of: 'if you sit on the river bank long enough, you see the bodies of your enemies float by'. I intended to stick around.

Y2: 7. Courtroom Scenarios

One source of stress came from my imagination being wrapped up in interview or (more commonly) courtroom scenarios. Inevitably the courtroom scenarios all involved me (or my barrister) picking holes in the prosecution's case. Mannheim and Linklee (or their absence) figured in many scenarios, but, as I had now been obliged to note, I had been surprised at every turn, never predicting events correctly. Thus I concluded that all this rumination served no purpose whatsoever, it was a total and utter waste of time. It did not lead anywhere and added nothing but stress to my day. Anxiety – the greatest inhibitor known to man.

The various interview room scenarios mated like rabbits producing curious hybrids, previously unknown to me. All tended to be negative. What had the police been doing for the nearly two years of investigation? Refining, honing their case like a butcher sharpened his knives? Were they making sure they were prepared to the infinite degree? Getting ready for the kill and keen to dazzle me with details and nuance lost to my memory? If the computer technician's report produced in the second police interview was indeed a preliminary report then a full comprehensive, detailed report should be available? If details were sprung on me in an interview or a courtroom while my head span, I feared I would be all over the shop which would doubtless suggest to the police or prosecutor that they were on to something. After all, if they had decided that they couldn't be bothered with all this, I would have heard something – 'No Further Action'. Good news travels fast, after all? The absence of news meant business, yes?

Thoughts therefore turned to my defence. What research could I undertake on Mannheim? Although I had witnessed her aggressive behaviour and the legal threats she had hurled down the phone at the car repair garage, I had little to go on. Running up and down the hills outside Oxford, I pondered my options. As I worked my way down the wooded path with her boyfriend's words ('this is what she does') echoing around my head, a thought popped into my mind. What if there had been others? What if research led to reports of not only aggressive behaviour but also to individuals who had suddenly found themselves arrested as a result of 'intelligence' received by the police. What if?

It was a long shot, but at least I might be able to demonstrate harassment and intimidation. I felt reasonably confident that I could track down the recipient of the aggressive phone call. I recalled that the phone call to the car repair garage had been made from the landline at Meadow Road, the bills for which I should have tucked away in storage somewhere.

Again, it was not only the literal, legal fight, but the psychological fight. Did I have the 'fight' in me? I knew from answering bail on numerous occasions I had no control of how I felt on any given day. I would arrive at work feeling sick at the thought of visiting the police station that day and wanting my solicitor to pass some information (however limited) to the police regarding Mannheim. The police might have established that there had been difficulties in the shared house but they might not have given it their full attention nor lent it the significance it deserved. But this urge was counter-balanced by a desire not to overrule my solicitor's professional advice. The constant swinging back and forth between strength and weakness was draining in itself. As far as I was concerned, there wasn't a snowball's chance in hell of me taking the rap, but one needed a certain amount of energy for a fight. I was not sure I had that energy.

Communicating with the solicitor's office after each re-bailing I was often encouraged to hear that they too seemed bewildered at the unusual delays. I could challenge it I was told, but I wasn't too fazed. I was too tired. Besides, perhaps the police were really delving deep into the housemates. If the matter was dropped, I might not learn the one thing I craved – the extent of my former housemates' involvement. As far as I was concerned, it wasn't about me, it was about my former co-tenants. So, perhaps it was best to leave it for the time being.

Over time I developed two strategic-psychological responses to my predicament: chill-and-breathe, or fight-and-spit. I could let events wash over me and roll with the blows and play the long game, or I could step up, be bolshy, bullish and seek to punch my way out of it. I wondered whether I should plan my strategy for both the police interview room and the courtroom ahead of time. Should they be the same? Or should one differ from the other? Would adopting one psychological strategy limit the use of another at a later date? Or would a strategy even be used against me at a later date? In fact did I have a choice? Would I try the cool, calm game only to lose my rag in the Crown Court?

'Mr Anderson, you don't seem very vexed with these allegations against you?' the smug prosecutor would say goading me, whereupon I would feel my blood rising and feel the need to make my point rather more forcefully than planned. Let them see how angry I am, I would think.

'Let me tell you what has been going on from my perspective, sir: on the 1st day I was indeed shocked and vexed. Similarly the 3rd day of my bail period I was rattled; likewise the 11th, 34th, 122nd, 178th, 234th or the day over a month after that on day 267, and day 299, day 304, day 343, day 387, 406, 489, 490, 492, 523, day 599, day 666, or even now day 721. Over 700 days have passed since the police visit and me being informed that 'intelligence' had been received about a possible offence. Each day has been different. Do you have a control group against which you can compare how an 'innocent man' would react on day 721? How do you know my reaction is not wholly compatible to that of a wronged man? If you intend to invoke psychology, then please do provide some science that could take the form of 'evidence'. Or [I would snort derisively] is 'evidence' not something you fancy bringing into this courtroom?'

Pleased with this particular courtroom scenario I banked it to my growing collection of courtroom responses, but wondered if it would be too strong. Too bolshy. Too arrogant. Would my defence counsel's insides be sinking as he/she silently begged me to stop?

[Note to Reader: the reference to 'day 721' above was correct at the time of first writing (drafting); in fact, I first appeared in court on day 899 for a hearing and the Crown Court trial was scheduled to start in the week of the third anniversary of my arrest, (i.e. day 1,091) but never took place. See Part Two for details.]

I considered the responses of those witnessing the exchanges in the courtroom (principally the jury). From their point of view, if I was in the dock there was a case to answer. Arguably, I might be seen as guilty until I proved my innocence. However, I believed that when the day came I could only respond to questions from my perspective, and my perspective centred wholly upon the housemates Mannheim and Linklee. If Mannheim had indeed been responsible directly or indirectly for the 'intelligence' then I could understand that she might not be referred to in discussions. However, if they were not the source of the intelligence then one would expect the police to establish who else had been in the house and had access to the computer. Surely? It would be a wholly legitimate line of questioning and investigation. To date there had been no information on the housemates, but perhaps further information would be available at a later date and all my ruminations would have gone to waste.

Watching a documentary about the sinking of the *Titanic* did not help ease a busy head. The documentary kept cutting to drama reconstructions of the inquest in New York following the disaster. A reconstruction of the inquest had a tough inquisitor drilling survivors for details of the events leading up to the sinking, asking short, serious questions and relentlessly pressing the witnesses on the spot, even limiting their words spoken in reply.

I wondered whether I would be given the chance to voice my opinions. Would the Crown Prosecutor ask short sharp questions and not allow me to elucidate? To give context? He, or she, would carefully phrase questions to damage my argument, pulling on years of courtroom experience to maximize my chances of losing my house, my employment (employability), friends, family and relationships past, present and future. There would be no aspect of my life that it would not touch. All of it wrapped up in perhaps ninety minutes.

No sooner had I considered this when I acknowledged once again that my imagined courtroom scenarios would not hit the mark. Accurate prediction had not been a strength during the previous eighteen months or so and had arguably been a tremendous waste of energy. It all made me feel weak.

On the last occasion of the year that I had spoken to DC Woods (in November) he had suggested that I not turn up at the station in person unless …. 'I phone you and then you can come in. And we can charge you, but we'll interview you first.'

What! WTF?!

His words had taken me completely by surprise.

There were no options? It wasn't between: charge, re-bail, No Further Action and interview (whereupon options are considered)? Just 'charge'. He had made up his mind? It was a formality? Something would definitely happen early in Year 3?

Y2: 8. Distractions

The distraction-routines had continued throughout the second year albeit overshadowed by thoughts of what day the news of my troubles would burst onto the outside-world-scene. I wondered whether my squash partner (of over ten years) would take a step back. Some acquaintances would, no doubt? The vigorous workouts of karate kept me sane, but I still avoided the 'family session' (ahead of the senior session). I was unsure how the club would have reacted if matters developed. Even though my Pickle was not a topic of conversation, that is not to say conversations did not hit upon the topic of my Pickle.

Attending training one Sunday morning, I was welcomed by fellow club members all of whom I had known for years and one of whom was a 22 year old student, Paige. She sidled up to me in a quiet moment in the session and asked how I was. I explained a recent injury and my recovery whereupon I asked about her summer holiday and imminent return to university.

'What year are you in now?' I asked. 'Entering your second year?'

'Third year.'

'Really? Wow. Time flies.'

'It's a four-year course though. Law.'

'Do you have to do the fourth year though?' I asked. 'Don't you get a degree after three years?'

'Yes.'

'But you may do a fourth year?'

'Maybe. To qualify as a solicitor.'

Previously Paige had never expressed an interest in legal work saying an office environment wasn't really for her. I understood.

'What would you like to do?' I asked.

'This,' she replied motioning at the dojo.

'Yep. Well, you should. No harm in qualifying as a solicitor though. Useful for all sorts of professions – business, civil service, public sector, government. You have to specialise though?'

'Yeah, I was thinking criminal law.'

'Right,' I nodded. Um, I gulped, reminded of my life as a suspect in a criminal case. It would be good to have an ally, I thought though; someone who could empathise with my progress through the criminal justice system. She would know soon enough. 'Crikey.'

'But my dad thinks no, I wouldn't like it.'

I nodded in acknowledgement. 'It isn't a pleasant business. It's even a miserable business.'

That said, people like me needed allies, I thought.

'Because,' she continued, 'I might have to end up defending a paedophile which would be rubbish.'

F*ck.

'So, naah,' she said shaking her head dismissively.

'Yeah,' I nodded.

F*ck.

I was apprehensive what words might tumble out of my mouth: 'But they might be innocent, or not have downloaded those images the police claim they did,' I didn't utter. I wondered whether the crashing and banging of the words as they bounced inside my head left a pained expression on my face.

Paige smiled and nodded, looking at the slightly ashen, middle-aged, balding man with raised eyebrows, no doubt thinking, 'that's curious'.

Another distraction was Spanish lessons, but I could withdraw from the evening classes with relative ease. News might never reach the students or tutors. DVD box-sets were a godsend pulling me into their fictional worlds, but largely failing to push me into my own – the physical act of writing was not possible. To write stories one needs to lull oneself into a creative slumber in the greenest of valleys, but for the time being there was a wolf loitering in 'them there woods'. It was dead time. A waiting game. I wished I could act on the words of Thomas Edison: 'everything comes to him who hustles while he waits'. I suspect Mr Edison had never found himself on police bail.

I was also kept busy by irregular activities including work events (both on-site and off-site) that were time consuming and involving. I was approached to make a short film for a local theatrical production. I accepted and used the steam-driven eMac left by police. I considered sending out screenplays and trying to develop interest in various projects, but struggled as I trembled in the fear that all might come crashing down nosily if legal events took an unpleasant turn. I did succumb to one film possibility that would not commit me (or rather expose me) to difficulties for many months and would allow me to withdraw discreetly in good time if necessary. A funding application (with a UK film producer and a Malaysian producer) for a co-production based on one of my stories was compiled and submitted to a regional agency, but I was keenly aware that everything I touched had to be built with get-out clauses.

A few film leads paid off. I received an email from a Soho-based producer wishing to discuss projects, so, in mid-September I travelled to Covent Garden with a handful of brochure materials not seized by the police eighteen months earlier. Having been warmly welcomed, the producer and I sat drinking coffee and talking about a few possible projects. I referred to the completed film (and the other 'in post-production') desperately hoping the conversation would not turn to a request to view any material. Although constructive, I felt exposed and realised that nothing could really proceed until I had the film materials back in my possession.

Nevertheless, seeds were planted and the meeting sparked a few ideas and the following week I was on the phone to a well-established film agent in central London with whom I had had a productive meeting two years earlier about developing a slate of projects. After the meeting I had gone away to develop scripts and ideas only for everything to grind to a halt with the police visit a few months later. I had subsequently kept a low-profile. Feeling there was no harm in re-establishing contact with the agent and explaining away the delays by referring to 'difficult times' in my personal life, I thought I might be able to reignite some negotiations. However, I learnt the film agent had moved on, changed careers and her replacement had not the time or inclination to follow up with me. Two years had passed and the momentum had been lost.

When in an unpleasant place, shopping is a widely recognised form of therapy, even the 'prospect of shopping' is recognised to be of benefit. Early in the year Apple introduced iPad – 'a revolutionary device for browsing the web, reading and sending email, enjoying photos, watching videos, listening to music, playing games, reading e-books and much more'. I still didn't have a computer and I didn't know if/when my Apple G4 would be returned by the police. I began to think of a new life with iPad in front of a woodburner in the new home with all the mod-cons. Eventually I succumbed and purchased a computer and an iPad, thinking I was probably being extravagant as the confiscated computer would surely be returned in a few months. Little did I know that, at (then) thirteen months in, I was not even halfway through the bail period.

Y2: 9. The Middle East

[Dear Reader, as I said in the Foreword I would give you a warning of a chapter describing a holiday break. So here is another. You are welcome to skip this chapter if you wish. It is of no (real) consequence to the story, but the three weeks away in Year Two was one helpful distraction in my thousand day-plus journey.]

While considering holiday options I had had one eye on visa applications looking for the particular question: 'have you ever been arrested?' I knew that visa applications for the USA listed a question along the lines of 'Have you ever been arrested or convicted for a crime that involved moral turpitude' and still of the opinion that my predicament was no accident, I wondered whether my nemesis had had just such a thing in mind knowing that an arrest alone would thwart any opportunities to follow up film or creative ambitions in the USA, for instance. If there ever came a time when the tables were turned and I was in a position to challenge Mannheim and Linklee, the removal of difficulty of visa applications to the USA would be 'a' (if not 'the') motivating factor.

On the day of departure I dragged my rucksack to work and bounced between meetings wearing my lightweight trousers and hiking boots. Leaving the office early on a beautiful, sunny, mid-afternoon I threw the rucksack over my shoulder and raced down the street to the bus station for my three-week escape. It started well with Heathrow having a little surprise for me. Queuing in economy, I was beckoned to a check-in desk off to the side to find myself being upgraded to Business Class on the flight to Damascus. It was the first time I had flown Business Class. It was almost as if someone or something was saying 'enjoy yourself, you deserve it'. (Maybe, feeling guilty, DC Woods had put in a good word?) Was it even a sign of things to come? Even a Business Class lounge is a tonic for life on police bail. An hour of free pastries and coffee and relative quiet was followed by complimentary champagne having boarded the aircraft, wider seats, more legroom, bigger TV screens and even metal knives and forks. Life was good and I was heading to a more peaceful part of the world. The Middle East.

By the time I landed in a sunny and soothing Damascus I was calm and clear-headed. During the course of the day I met the tour group of two Americans (a male from San Francisco and female from Washington D.C.), two Irishmen, a retired Australian couple and an Australian lawyer. A few of us headed to the mosque and the Saladin shrine followed by some shopping. I met a very friendly carpet-seller Mike in the souk and, after much chat, I promised to return another day to buy a carpet. (He was, after all, going to give me a very good price because he liked me, apparently.) On Saturday afternoon I returned to the hotel to rest before meeting our tour guide, Bashar, in the evening. A very nice, humble, good-natured chap, Bashar was our guide for the Syria-leg before handing us over to another guide at the Jordanian border the following week. Every evening Bashar would give a half-hour talk on Syrian history or culture and his plans to marry later that year.

That first evening Bashar walked us to a restaurant in the old city where the group watched World Cup football and bonded.

The next morning we caught a train to the city of Aleppo in the north of the country. Dozing on the train whizzing through sunny Syrian countryside I could feel my body relax. A walking tour of Aleppo and its fabulous, ancient souk followed, before a visit to the Citadel and the mosque in the uncomfortable heat. Heading to the bar Bashar and I watched England lose 4-1 to Germany.

The following day we left for a day trip to St Simeon's Church. Though largely a ruin, the fifth century church was still impressive. The base of the column (around which the church had been built) on which St Simeon had sat for thirty-seven years remained. The afternoon included a tour of the old city and its local businesses including a soap factory. The evening was spent on a roof-top restaurant overlooking Aleppo chatting to my new American and Irish friends and watching the Brazil-Chile game. Asked of my life in the UK, I spoke of the film, but limited the development of the conversation when it came to the film's distribution.

We left Syria's second city in a larger air-conditioned bus and drove to Hama, a mid-sized city. I made a point of indulging in one of my loves: sitting in the front seat of a vehicle in sunglasses and zoning out for hours as I watched the vista (in widescreen) roll past – straight empty roads, undulating landscapes, unnameable vegetation. The air-conditioned air fought the heat trying to beat its way into the vehicle from the road and sun. With my feet up on the dashboard, sipping warm water and nibbling unfamiliar snacks, it was the greatest of balms. There was nothing for me to do, just relax in peace and quiet with like-minded curious people from around the planet.

We stopped at Hama for a few hours and visited the water wheels 'norias' used for irrigation. The deep moaning of the massive wooden wheels as they turned, straining under their considerable weight, echoed across the city; the sound was both haunting and majestic, like a wounded medieval dragon. Back on the bus we travelled to Krak des Chevaliers and the group opted for lunch in a hill-top restaurant ahead of a tour of the castle itself. Served a sumptuous salad lunch by a jolly, pink-shirted, portly, multi-lingual, middle-aged man, we relished the cool insides of the establishment ahead of the two-hour tour of the castle in blistering heat.

Mid-week, we drove to Palmyra in the barren and rocky desert, beyond which lies Iraq. Arriving at the hotel we learnt that Roger Federer had lost at Wimbledon to Tomas Berdych upsetting Bashar. We visited the ruins of Palmyra (first a settlement dating to 2,000 BC before becoming a major centre for trade in the first two centuries AD) and marvelled at its arches and colonnades – witnesses to lost crowds. In the cool of the late afternoon we watched the sun set on the region from a nearby citadel. The following day we visited the tower tombs outside Palmyra before returning to Damascus and a tour of its old city and later a tour to three monasteries outside the city. Lost deep in the souk at the end of the day I came across a lamp shop with window full of colour and illumination. I learnt the lamps were covered with broken glass glued on to a carbon fibre frame. My new home in the UK needed a bit of colour and I soon concluded that a lamp would serve as an affectionate reminder of the gentle Syrian people. I picked up two lamps for 6,000 Syrian pounds. Aware posting the lamps back to the UK would be too costly, I committed myself to carrying them for the following two weeks through Jordan and Egypt. A return visit to Mike the carpet-seller would not be possible therefore; it would be a home furnishing too far. For our final night in

Damascus Bashar led us to a splendid restaurant complete with a whirling dervish show.

From Damascus we headed to Amman in Jordan stopping off for a few hours at the city of Bosra which hosted the best preserved Roman amphitheatre in the world – enormously impressive with superb acoustics. In Amman our group expanded to include more Canadians and more Australians. What we gained in numbers, we lost in intimacy. Our tour leader, Ossama, gave us a tour of the city including the Citadel and Jarash, the best preserved Roman city in the world before we jumped into a van for the two hour trip to the Dead Sea. After a short soak and float, we were on the road again. The day ended with an evening talking about excursions in Egypt and watching the Netherlands-Uruguay game.

Having lotioned-up in Petra Visitors' Centre and walked twenty minutes through the gorge, we arrived at the Treasury. Although the low season, the area was swarming with tourists who appeared to spend most of their time with their backs turned to the monument in order to face a camera device that could record the moment. Walking deeper into the Petra valley I was surprised by the scale of the abandoned city – yet more Roman colonnades and streets. A twenty-five minute power-walk led me up to the Monastery before a return to the valley permitted a brief visit to the basilica. The heat claimed my will to explore further and I wound down. After Petra we drove to Wadi Rum and spent the night in a Bedouin camp, snatching the opportunity to watch the Germany-Spain game.

After a two hour jeep tour the following morning the tour moved to Aqaba for a walk on the beach. On Friday we transferred to Dahab in Egypt (via the port at Nuweiba) and met our guide for the Egypt-leg, Khalid. I had expected Dahab to be much like Aqaba (hot with lots of hanging around), but no, the Egyptian resort was a pleasant surprise with cafes and little tourist shops lining the sea-front. Hours were lost collapsed on cushions drinking coffee and reading, all the while being both warmed by the sun beating its way through flapping awnings and cooled by the breeze off the sea. After a morning of snorkelling the following day, we jumped into the van and drove to a hotel in the Sinai retiring early at 9.00 p.m.

Rising at 1.30 a.m. we left the hotel and travelled to the bottom of Mount Sinai for 2.30 a.m. and a two and a half hour climb to the summit under a crystal clear Milky Way. Reaching the summit with a hundred other tourists we watched the sun rise (behind a cloud) before climbing down the mountain as the day warmed to reach St Catherine's monastery by eight o'clock. A small group of us hung around the doors hoping to gain access to visit the tree from which God had spoken to Moses, but without any luck. Even the words of a fifty-something group member (travelling overseas for the first time) failed to impress whoever it was behind the door: 'We're Canadian,' but no, she was denied access along with the rest of us.

Back to the hotel we packed up, loaded the van and began our long drive across the Sinai, along the Suez canal to Cairo. The pyramids of Giza loomed out of the haze on the way to the hotel. I had visited Egypt as a student twenty years before and was keen to return just to drink in the spectacle once again. As a nineteen year old the world was my oyster. The future was bright and exciting, full of movies and magic. I had a taken a picture (a 'selfie') in front to the pyramids that I had wanted to recreate (and compare with my present-day 'self'). Giza creates a sense of the unreal and timeless, so the romantic in me had the present-day traveller meeting his (or rather 'my') younger self wandering about the Giza site. I wondered whether my younger self would recognise my older self. The younger self might excitedly share his plans for the 1990s and the 2000s. 'How's that working out for 'me'?' he might ask. How should the older man reply? There are some things a young man should never know, one of them being his future.

In Cairo, the group was splitting up and evolving. Some new friends were leaving, other new people were joining. The final night of the original Syrian tour group was spent watching the world cup final (Spain v. Netherlands) in the hotel's rooftop bar.

Monday morning was spent at the Giza site. I took my selfie and wandered around in respectful silence. On Monday evening the enlarged group took an overnight train to Luxor. I had also visited the Valley of the Kings twenty years before, but I had missed the tour of the Karnak temple and Hippolyte Hall on my previous visit owing to illness, so I was pleased to honour the decades-old promise to myself to visit the temple. The following evening the tour group prepared to travel on to Aswan while a small remnant of the Jordan tour group returned to Cairo on the overnight train. I spent the last day of the holiday packing (checking the state of the Damascus lamps), shopping and having a 50 pence haircut. I was at the airport by late afternoon and flew back economy class to Heathrow.

The three weeks in the Middle East had served their purpose. It was a break from the rubbish, injected some perspective (a degree of which I already had, but the trip acted as an steroid-like enhancer). The most effective days at giving perspective were the visits to the sites of Palmyra, Bosra, Petra and Giza. All had evidence of a great civilisations passing away into dust. The work required to build and maintain the structures over centuries would have been huge, involving considerable numbers of people. There was not one person (even several generations removed) who could report on the life-story of any person involved in the construction or maintenance of any of those communities now in ruin. Similarly I was aware that no living human had witnessed the nineteenth century; all the dusty ruins of my Middle East tour thrived over a millennium before that – ancient cities full of people with lives far more dramatic than my own. Three weeks was a healthy reminder. One needs to take the big picture. Let's get this Pickle over and move on.

If pressed to identify any moments within those days (selected above) that articulated this argument, there were two: Petra and Giza. Halfway through the tour of Petra a donkey brayed. The sound echoed around the peaceful, rock-enclosed valley filling it with a deafening noise of 'life'. In its heyday Petra had one thousand caravans of merchants and visitors arriving a year – an average of nearly three a day. The ancient city would have had thousands of animals and tens of thousands of people milling about at any one time. My guess was that the sound of a bustling Petra in its prime would have been louder than anything experienced in the world today. Louder than anything an eighty-thousand-seat sports stadium could muster. Now the city of rock was largely silent, bar the odd donkey's bray.

The Giza complex had developed considerably in the twenty years since my visit. In 1989 one could just wander up from the Giza settlement to the pyramids themselves. It was open and available to all. Now there are walls and gates and a visitors' centre. On my return visit I took the opportunity to visit a museum at the base of the pyramids which housed an exhibition of an ancient Egyptian boat found flat-packed and tucked under dozens of 17-20 ton limestone slabs under the side of the pyramid of Cheops. The museum housed the reconstructed boat in all its glory. At 142 feet long, by nearly 20 feet wide, it is a fully functioning boat said to have been built to carry the Pharoah across the heavens. It is the oldest boat on the planet at 4,500 years. Would any boat built (or even manuscript written) today be found intact and working in the year 6,510 AD (itself a date over four thousand years after the USS Starship Enterprise is scheduled to be exploring the frontiers of space)?

It was difficult to imagine the thousands of craftsmen who designed, built and buried the ancient craft. Each man had a life-story. With these kinds of timescales (and 'life-story-scales') in my head, it was difficult to lend too much weight to my own predicament. The worst that could happen after a worst-case scenario was a criminal charge; after which any sentencing would be worked through in fifteen months.

Year Three (Y3)

Y3: 1. It's Life, Jim

'So, here we are – the third calendar year of psychological incarceration. What would this year bring?' I asked myself as January arrived. It was life, of sorts, but not as I had known it.

Reviewing my predictions for the previous year, each one had been inextricably woven into the fabric of the Pickle. It touched everything – job, home, family, finances, relationships (with everything and everybody), physical health, psychological well-being. At that time (twelve months earlier) I had been three weeks away from answering bail for a fifth time (which was following up the second police interview). Of course, the January meeting never happened and nor had anything since. Therefore here I was a year later and nearly five weeks away from the eleventh time I was being required to answer bail.

The words of the police officer manning the reception counter in July of Year 2 were never far away from my thoughts: 'we think we are reaching the end of our investigation', but nothing had happened when I had answered bail the following October. In November, DC Woods had referred to charging me (albeit interviewing me first), so the likelihood of a development in my story was increasing. As I approached each day to answer bail it had become customary to list the probability of interview, charge or other. As Year 2 had begun I had conservative estimates: interview 65% ; re-bail 25% ; No Further Action 10%. Later in Year 2 the odds had been: interview, 90%; re-bail, 7%; No Further Action, 3%. But as I entered the third year of psychological incarceration was that a good sign or a bad sign? Should the odds go up or down?

The madness.

By the time I was due to answer bail for an eleventh time I settled on 98-99 per cent likelihood of an interview with 98-99 per cent likelihood of criminal charges to follow. I retained one or two per cent for an alternative, but I had no idea what it could be. I was now both wise and cynical. ('Wisdom' and 'cynicism' – the two words were now comfortable bed-fellows.)

In the meantime there was a lull for five weeks. I say 'lull', it was more like the writhing of a man suspended at the end of a rope. Delayed closure, perhaps. I returned to the office after New Year. In meetings my employer nodded solemnly as he laid out his plans for me to take on more work and responsibility. I reciprocated the nodding and agreed the future was exciting. I had managed to push through the creation of a new post in my 'unit'. Little did my employer know that I was laying the groundwork for my sudden departure.

I was aware (and grateful, I suppose) that the day job provided some structure and routine to the extended bail periods. Nevertheless I needed to make a conscious effort to manage the 'suspense' or 'stress', otherwise, it would end up managing me. In my circumstances I could not engage in any long term planning. This was one of the fundamental problems of such bail periods. One could only 'plan' for four, six or eight weeks in advance (those being the usual bail periods). Because the police could keep extending bail without any recourse to a court, it could go on for years. (The following year there was some discussion in the media of limiting the period on police bail, but only because 'famous' people had found themselves on police bail for a staggering six or even (an incomprehensible) twelve months.)

The early part of the new year brought renewals of membership for various associations and clubs. I was handed a sports club annual membership form, it asked the question:

have you ever been convicted of or charged with a serious crime / offence? Technically, on that particular day, the answer had been 'no'. I could sign the form with a clear conscience. However, I noted that ninety-six hours later all that could change, so I took the opportunity to complete and return the form on the spot.

Similarly later in the year I logged on the price comparison websites to research house insurance renewals. I noted that the online form asked the question(s): 'Do any members of the household have a criminal conviction? Or have a prosecution pending?' Once again, I didn't have a conviction and I didn't have a prosecution pending – just then. Thirteen days later I might not have been be able to claim such a privileged status. I had trouble completing the online form to process the renewal, so phoned a number and ended up speaking to Nathan. He asked various questions, but did not mention the criminal conviction question; no matter, I had a reply ready that I could have delivered with sincerity. However, he did rattle through miscellaneous conditions including one which stated that should any of the conditions or answers change during the course of the insurance period, I should contact them immediately otherwise my policy might be declared void. Yeah right, I thought. Nathan didn't dwell on it and continued to rattle through his script while my mind lingered on one matter. I didn't raise the hypothetical situation pressing on my mind (it was nearly 7.00 p.m. on a Friday evening and he probably had plans), but I did speculate about a telephone conversation, say, sixteen days later:

'Hello, the conditions for the recent house insurance policy may have changed.'

'Okay, thank you, what would that be?'

'I now have a criminal prosecution pending.'

'Oh. Right. Okay. Really. Um, can you tell me what the prosecution is for?' the operator would ask a little less nonchalantly. I imagined s/he would be expecting a speeding fine and three points on my licence, or the failure to buy a television licence.

'Downloading indecent images of children,' I say chirpily down the phone.

'Oh. Okay.'

There's a pause. Perhaps s/he is waiting for me to say I was only joking.

'But it wasn't me, I'm innocent. Honest.'

More silence down the other end, so I decide to make light of it, 'but I suppose they all say that, don't they?' I chuckle.

'I need to consult my supervisor. I'll put you on hold.'

'Of course, sure. Thank you very much.'

Y3: 2. Mental Health

Standing at the bus stop on the way home from work one evening, I listened to Simon Mayo's radio show's banter about whether a full moon could affect people's moods. The moon's gravity influenced tides, the mating habits of crabs and human physiology. There was discussion of whether more crimes were committed during a full moon, which got me thinking about whether the moon could have an influence on brain chemistry. If the moon could move oceans, why couldn't it influence neuro-chemicals thus influencing the 'ocean of the mind'? Was calmness (or irritation for that matter) in part dependent on the time of the month? Would the timing of the police interview in the lunar calendar influence my own state of mind and perhaps those interviewing and advising me? But it wasn't all about interview or courtroom scenarios, I feared for my sanity as I mulled over my troubles while on a bus full of commuters and becoming increasingly vexed as I sat in front of two passengers talking spectacularly inane stuff about Charlie Sheen.

I was becoming aware of the helpful influence of music to soothe my troubled soul. The tracks' lyrics spoke to me and rarely failed to restore the fight deep inside. I compiled a 'Crazy Pickle' playlist of songs to which I turned when times were tough. The songs either inspired me for any upcoming 'fight' or their lyrics lent themselves to my predicament and were soothing to some degree.

Occasionally I was reminded that my psychology was visible to the outside world. I would catch reflections of myself in shop windows and see no smile, pleasure, just anxiety stretched taut across pale features. Any sense of peace had been bled from my veins almost as if Mannheim had slit my wrists letting it bleed away. On one occasion, shortly after I returned from a holiday, I played squash with my long-time squash partner, Ryan, (who was particularly upbeat) fifteen hours before a scheduled 'interview'.

'Last week you were a bit sullen,' he said, 'so I didn't press you for news on your holiday as I knew you were struggling with being back to the office'.

'Oh yeah, right,' I said, thinking that was previous week I had returned to the UK eight days before another scheduled 'interview'.

'Tell me about your holiday,' he had asked.

'No, well, yeah, I'm still struggling with being back in the office, ' I had muttered in reply.

But the one time I really did struggle and it was apparent for all to see was eighteen months into my bail period. An older, Sydney-based brother, Andrew, visited the UK for a few weeks and visited my new home four days before I was due to answer bail (for the ninth time and after 610 days on police bail). Usually the two-week countdown to answering bail at the police station, was never pretty, but being ninety-six hours away from a third interview, I was not in the best of shape. Suffering a stress headache and having thrown up during the morning, I opened the front door to play host to the visit from 12.30 p.m. He knew nothing, but my mother, who was accompanying him, knew everything.

After muted 'Hellos' I explained that I was not feeling too good. (I thanked the gods that I had been throwing up earlier in the morning so I could say so with a clear conscience.) I explained that it was probably tiredness and too much computer at which my mother expressed concern that I was working too hard. My brother, however, struck another note – was I stressed?

'Because stress could sometimes induce headaches,' he said.

If only he knew, but I wasn't going to go there today, I thought.

Moving into the kitchen, I started making coffee as we continued to talk work and tiredness. They didn't know the half of it. Or rather Andrew didn't and started talking about jobs and options not aware that I would almost certainly be charged (or so I thought at the time) for a criminal offence 96 hours later; a charge that limited all possible options and killed reputations.

Andrew talked about being positive and shared his own experiences. It was like being punched on the chin repeatedly with 'good advice' without any means to block the well-meaning and well-targeted fists. I just had to smile, nod and take the beating, but like any barrage of well-meaning punches, my chin was wobbling and I found myself pinching the bridge of my nose and rubbing my eyes as I mumbled 'yes' and acknowledged all the sound advice pounding my face. My mother also offered a few words of advice, but I suspected that she knew that it was the upcoming event (answering bail) that was pressing on my mind.

'Is it because of Wednesday?' she whispered as my brother nipped to the kitchen to add more milk to his coffee.

I mumbled in the affirmative.

'Have you heard anything?'

'No.'

'Has anything changed?'

'No,' I mumbled shaking my head shielding my eyes.

'Why don't you tell him?'

'No,' I said. My head hurt. What would I say? Explain how and why the police were nipping at my heels? I didn't know myself.

'Why don't you show Andrew your garden?' my mother suggested once we were all together.

'What? Why? It's just patch of land.'

'He would want to see it.'

Anything for a quiet life. I led the way outside, but by then my chin was going. I fiddled with the latch on the gate. As I pathetically struggled to loosen its catch, its resistance mirrored my lack of composure. As the mechanism wobbled, so my sanity and composure was wobbling. Fortunately, my 'feeling rough this morning' story was proving to be a useful cover.

I led the way across the neighbour's patch of garden and through another gate to my little plot of land almost the size of a tennis court.

'This is it,' I said waving my hand at my little crappy, overgrown empire, but unable to meet my brother's eyes. It was lunchtime, I hadn't drunk or eaten anything that morning. I was soon to be rearrested and charged with a criminal offence and the next part of my life would begin to gracefully disintegrate like a spaceship caught in the gravitational pull of a black hole at the end of a bad movie.

'God you look awful,' my brother said catching sight of my profile. 'Your eyes are all red.'

I breathed out unable to counter or excuse the observation. The fight had gone. I felt like a stunned cattle in an abattoir.

There were a few seconds of silence. I sensed a movement to my side and without a word, I felt his arms wrap around me. No words. I stood there motionless and silent.

'Let's go in,' he said guiding me to the gate. I shuffled like a broken, old man back to the house. My insides had been lost to the gravity of the situation. Everything felt as if it was falling earthwards never to rise again. My eyes, the muscles in my cheeks drooped south, my mouth had fallen open, my shoulders dropped, my heart, stomach dragged along the floor, my feet just managed to break free of the pathway for the briefest of moments as I moved my myself forwards.

Back in the kitchen we resumed our positions – me leaning against the sink as the conversation resumed to how I should change my job, get something more stimulating. My brother returned to the subject of taking a positive mental attitude through which one could bring about change.

Yeah, right. No idea.

To be fair Andrew did ask was there something else going on in my life. Was I ill, he asked.

'No.' I shook my head and muttered that I was fine.

We talked more and I continued to rub the bridge of my nose as if it would release a genie. I was asked if I wanted to head back to my parents that evening, but no, I needed a day to relax. I waved them off promising to drop by the following day for Sunday lunch.

I received a few odd looks in Sainsbury's that afternoon. I've no doubt that I looked rough, but I was beyond caring. During the afternoon I struggled to doze, watched television almost wondering when and how I'd escape the struggle. The following day, Sunday, I woke relatively refreshed to a beautiful sunny day and, as promised, headed to Sunday lunch with my parents, Andrew and another brother, Joseph. Bizarrely, I felt calm and relaxed even though I was twenty-four hours nearer the bail date. Was it because the sickness had bled out some of the toxicity or was it a sign of things to come? Was I hormonal? Was something going on with the investigation and I was picking up through my sixth sense? ('Mr David has good sixth sense.') With all this turning over in my mind, what kind of mood would I be in on the day of interview itself? The 'Saturday fretfulness' or the 'Sunday chill'? How would that impact my interview strategy for the day? Should my strategy be based upon the mood of the day?

I had a fact bouncing about my head that the human heart had set number of heartbeats available to it. Having noted that I had been using up many additional beats in the previous few years, it was fair to assume my Pickle was literally shortening my life. Sometimes my heart was in a continuously-edgy-pounding state for no obvious reason. One occasion was curious – in late February in Year 3. Since the eleventh re-bailing (on 2 February) I had maintained an essentially positive feeling, but on the evening of 28 February from nowhere I very suddenly developed a violent edginess while watching television. Was something going on? Was I tapping into something beyond my every-day senses?

Y3: 3. Witness for the Prosecution

A few days later, when I dropped by my parents on the way to an evening of de-stressing sport, things took a peculiar turn. As I prepared a cup of tea at the kitchen sink, my mother took her seat at the kitchen table with the words, 'Chris Woods seems nice'.

I recognised the name, Chris Woods. It took me a moment to place it however. I processed my thoughts – not only: how does she know his name, but how would she know whether DC Chris Woods was nice or not? They had never met.

I expressed my confusion.

'He came yesterday. Knocked on the door, came in for a chat,' she said.

In a blurry few minutes I learnt that DC Woods had visited and had a long chat with my father after which they were joined by my mother. I struggled to take the news in. I had thought things were winding down. What the hell was the detective doing knocking on my parents' door when, in theory, the investigation was reaching a conclusion?

'What did he want?' I asked.

'He wanted to know if I used the computer,' my father replied, 'and wanted to know what happened on the day the police visited.'

It got worse.

My father happily announced that he was asked for a written statement saying that he hadn't used the computer and was also asked whether he would testify in court (that he hadn't used the computer).

What the hell?

'What else?' I asked, aghast.

My father explained that he then 'had a go' at the police for the two years his son had been on police bail and insisted that he (me, his son) had been 'set up' having had problems with former housemates.

I wondered whether DC Woods had taken that onboard. 'Did you say anything else? Give their names?'

'Ian and his German girlfriend,' came the reply.

I had visions of police now approaching Mannheim and her saying whatever she liked: 'Have you tried the suspect's brother, Joseph? He used the computer. Or other family members too?'

'Did Joe use the computer?' my mother asked.

'Anybody who came to the house used it to check email, train times, or review sequences of the edited movies.'

I became increasingly irritated and nauseous. Fuck. How did this happen? I had a sense of a complete lack of control. A toxin was creeping back into my veins infecting my muscles, my heart, my lungs. I tried to expel its poison, but trying to clear my lungs only polluted the air around me and I was left to inhale and ingest it again.

'You have to write it down,' I kept repeating. 'We need a record of everything that was said before you forget. I need to advise my solicitor.'

'He was nice,' my mother kept saying. 'We told him you were advised to say 'no comment' at the interview. I don't trust solicitors. They're all liars.'

WTF.

'He was the police,' I protested.

'But he was nice. I trust him more that I trust the solicitor who advised you to say no comment,' my mother protested in return, becoming defensive and agitated herself.

What?

'DC Chris Woods was here to gather information – to solicit statements to strengthen their case,' I said. 'They will twist and portray anything you say as they see fit. Just as they had done with me.'

My father chipped in, trying to lessen the tension, but failing miserably.

'We had a good chat. He was only here to take a statement saying I wasn't on the computer. He said sometimes the police feel bad because they think they need to arrest everybody in the house.'

What were they thinking? My parents were going to testify against me.

'Why didn't you call me?'

'We didn't think,' my mother replied. 'But he was nice.'

Holy fuck.

Maybe the Crown Prosecution Service had told the nice DC Woods that they needed a form of words isolating me as the sole user, forget anything else (including trouble with other housemates).

When I suggested that it sounded as if my father had agreed to act as a witness for the prosecution my parents pooh-poohed the idea – 'don't be ridiculous, we were being supportive'.

Perhaps I was being paranoid.

I didn't want to go on the sports training session. I felt sick and just wanted to go home, but I knew I would feel sick all evening pacing about the house. A bit of exercise would do me good. I continued to make my drink amidst the tension in the kitchen and retired to the sitting room and stared at the walls. It was just like the early days of police bail – acute tension and frustration. I thought I had become accustomed to being the bailed pornographer (alleged). I could tell my mother was irritated by my reaction. Perhaps she was expecting gratitude that they had had a nice chat defending their son and laying the groundwork for a desirable solution.

And there you have it. A relatively calm, bailed sex offender (alleged) one minute, then 'the police are nice, lawyers are liars' and my father a witness for the prosecution the next. I thought I had worked through all the possible scenarios. Where was this one? I hadn't seen this coming. Never.

I went to sports training and had a decent session considering the early evening's events, but I was aware I was wearing my 'grumpy, fierce, don't talk to me' face. Later at home I noted that, although feeling better for the exercise, my overall well-being had taken a giant leap backwards.

Y3: 4. Family and Friends

I was reminded that my troubles were not all about the strain on my mind and body. It was also a strain for family members and on familial relationships and friendships. This bugged me because I was all too aware that all the hullabaloo had been ultimately prompted by the so called 'intelligence' received by police. Even after two years on bail I had yet to be advised on the nature and content of the intelligence. Yet, whatever its source, the ramifications of the receipt of that 'intelligence' were now affecting family members directly and seeping into family relationships. My mother had often reminded me that my predicament was just as worrying and stressful for them as parents. They had wanted to tell my three brothers and sister, but I had always said no. Partly on the advice of my solicitor on the day of arrest, but also because I had wanted to wait until there was something (anything) to report. If there was no prospect of further developments (sometimes for months) the matter could be put in a box and stuck in the corner of the attic. Broaching the matter with friends and family (and its awkward conversations) would only serve to keep the matter front and centre in my head. No, those conversations with family could wait, besides maybe the matter would dissolve once the police had investigated the German connection.

On the day following the witness-for-the-prosecution conversation there was no interaction with my parents, which was odd considering the unresolved discussions of the previous night. I suspected my mother was making a point of not communicating, because of my brittleness at learning of the visit from the 'nice' police detective. And so, sitting in my VW

Golf in the ring road car park after work, I phoned home. I apologised for my agitation on Wednesday and listened to my father's attempts to soothe my concerns about the visit and my predicament as a whole. He did reveal one detail of interest. Apparently the detective had said that they were finding it difficult to 'pin down what happened'. I supposed what the police were in fact saying was that they were having difficulty pinning it on me. Perhaps they hadn't seriously considered the alternative or were taking any statement from Mannheim as gospel.

I learnt no further details about the conversation, other than it went on for one to one and a half hours! I imagined DC Woods sitting there quietly nodding as my mother refilled his tea cup and supplied more carrot cake while my father rambled on inadvertently laying out the groundwork for his son to be sent to a high-security prison for 25 years.

I decided not to suggest to my father again that which had been playing on my mind, namely that he might be called upon to act as a witness for the prosecution, but he brought it up anyway. He reported that he had emphasised to the detective that far from being a witness for the prosecution he would be very supportive of me. I listened as he talked in the way a father should and any son would appreciate in hindsight. Fuck. What a mess.

In the knowledge that our conversation was eating into my 100 minute mobile phone allowance we signed off after half-an-hour. I needed to deal with that another day, but I did conclude with the words 'apologise to mother for the other night'.

'No need to apologise,' replied my father perhaps almost believing it himself.

Then there was the issue of visiting family members, but the thought of visiting them and trying to relax and chat was stressful in itself.

'Come up anytime,' was a regular refrain over the phone from my sister or her husband and it reared its ugly head again after the birth of a niece. Yeah right, I would think each time. Did I visit having been charged with a criminal offence? How would I explain? It was not so much the feared awkwardness but the constant deceit that was debilitating. Setting up the first Skype video-conference call between my Sydney-based brother and my parents at their home was typical. With me sitting at the computer in front of the camera and my parents behind me, we connected successfully.

'Any news?' my brother cheerfully asked as an opener.

'No,' we all lied and sighed in unison. It was all lies, lies, lies. Not conventional lies where somebody benefited such as the denial of eating the last cake, the stealing of a car or pushing a little old lady into the canal. No, these were bad lies like the desperate gasps of a drowning man about everything being 'okay'. Lies where nobody benefited.

My troubles affected friendships too. I had taken a similarly cautious approach of keeping friends at bay as I waited for news to emerge. The practice of stepping back had been initiated when there was just four months to wait before the police would reveal all and it only continued when the waiting was extended by a matter of six or eight weeks each time. I had never thought it would repeat itself thirteen times over nearly two and a half years.

In the Spring of Year 3 I met Irfan, a Malaysian film friend I had first met at a film market in 2007. We discussed a film funding submission that we had made earlier in the year which looked as if it would not be successful. Nevertheless, there were other projects we could work on. He asked about the marketing of my completed film. I fudged it with a smile, a sigh and a wave of the hand choosing not to share with him that it had been sitting in a police lock-up for years. He, however, seemed to be doing well which was nice. [Sigh]

On another occasion I bumped into an old work boss, Matthew, in the street. As we caught up I was reminded that if/once charged (and the matter became public record) I would need to have a number of awkward conversations with people like Matthew (who had also acted as a referee for my current work position). In fact, I noted, there might come a time when I might have to ask him to act as a referee once again – for my character from the witness stand in a Crown Court. As Matthew and I talked and I nodded politely and smiled, I was thinking that he might well hear a few months later about aspects of my life omitted from our conversation. Perhaps he would read about it in the local newspaper and reflect on our exchange in the street that day and think, 'I'd never have thought'.

With all the strain on family and social circles I reflected on how my two-plus years of troubles were changing me and would change me regardless of the (legal) result. If I saw it through, would I be harder, more cynical, colder, less trusting as an individual? I anticipated being less trusting of the police certainly – not only their motives but their competency as public 'servants'.

Y3: 5. Sanity in the Madness

As time went on, each and every small thing took on some sort of significance. Everything was pickled. Roundabout this time I logged on to my work email account to find an email ostensibly from my personal email account with a link to a Canadian drugs website. My personal email account had been compromised. A contact in my address book emailed me confirming as much. I was relieved it was drugs and nothing more troubling, but it reminded me that these things did happen. I made a point of keeping such emails as evidence. I might be able to refer to it in court.

As each day on which I was required to answer bail approached I looked for other signs: driving to work shortly before answering bail for an eleventh time I had a straight run sailing through the traffic lights, no stopping anywhere. What was going on? Did it mean I was going to 'sail through' the following Wednesday?

In the absence of information from the police, I had been looking for patterns, guidance, signs. Interviews to date had been conducted 'in the darkness' – towards the end of the day in the winter months: 4.00 p.m. on the day of arrest (February) and 5.30 p.m. on the day of the second police interview (December). I had only ever emerged from an interview blinking in the blackness. On the occasions I had been required to answer bail during the summer months I had been re-bailed and any 'interview' postponed. Therefore – summertime, good; wintertime, bad.

The most tense time was around the transition to British Summer Time when I didn't know what to think. On one occasion forty-eight hours before answering bail at 6.00 p.m. in February a work colleague popped her head into my office.

'Look,' she said, 'it's 4.45 p.m. and it's still light.'

Yes, I thought. Things were looking brighter. If only I could be re-bailed for a twelfth time then it boded well until at least the winter closed in at the end of the year.

There were more signs pointing my way through the madness. As I cycled to work I spotted a roadsign announcing roadworks near my workplace. Within a few days the tarmac outside the building had been pulled up and, within two or three nights, re-laid. This wasn't a pothole, this was a whole new intersection. Interesting. Spooky. The very next day I drove home and the road into my market town (previously closed for resurfacing roadworks) had reopened – after four weeks and not the advertised six weeks! The world was going crazy.

During April there were loads of road repairs. Halfway along the A338 to Wantage the country road swung around a bend between two old mill-houses each perched right on the road's edge. For the previous year I had had to swing the car into the centre of the road (oncoming traffic permitting) to avoid two long disintegrating cracks along both sides of the road's edge. Whichever way I was travelling my car's wheels would be hammered if I mistimed my approach. Returning home one day I found both cracks had disappeared under a warm, dark grey, beautifully smooth, smudge of honey. I almost guided my car into the edges of the road to run my passenger side wheels along their length. For the previous twelve months I had taken my eyes off the traffic to guide my vehicle through the broken chasms that had screamed my life was broken, all hope was lost. Not now. Coincidence? I thought not.

And there were more, two in particular. On one evening I drove down the slip road onto a ring-road to be met by a sign saying a lane would be closed for part of the day for emergency repairs. Lo and behold, a monster indentation (nearly 1.5 times the size of a full-size ironing board) had been filled in. Secondly, driving home late one night I rounded the corner on to my own road (fifty yards from home) ready to undertake the manoeuvre to avoid a loaf-sized-deep hole in the tarmac, but there was no need – because it had been repaired! WTF?

Pot-holes, elongated cracks, in fact all road hazards formed part of the galaxy as much as any flower, asteroid or photon. If the cosmos saw fit to fix them (and on my watch), job done. 'Nuff said. Broken things had been made good. It must have been a sign of things to come.

My morning run took me along a path beside a busy road beside which a high bank of vegetation (wild grass, weeds and other 'stuff') grew. As the warm weather approached cow parsley bloomed and overhung the path forcing me to step into the road on a busy bend. As I struggled past the cow parsley, I wondered whether the cosmos would step up and arrange for the pruning of the overhang – to clear and smooth my path (literal and legal). A form of road repair. Within a week and as the thirteenth occasion on which I was required to answer bail approached (Year 3: April) I found the path bordered by beautifully pruned cow parsley permitting an undisturbed end of my run. Perhaps I was not without a few allies. A path through my troubles would be cleared in time.

Y3: 6. Re-bailing Routines Pt 1

Besides watching for patterns in the sky and the world about me, I was now familiar with the pattern of answering bail. At fourteen days before a visit to the police station there was a noticeable shift of gear – psychological and physiological. Daily life became particularly fretful and anxiety-riven although no-one looking at me would have known it. As each night drew in I would start to pace about the house trying to make notes. The anxiety was not so much the prospect of an interview or appearance in a court, but the anticipation of what people would think and how to broach the matter with family and work colleagues. I was conscious that different people might react to the news. On one occasion my office door was opened by a work colleague (a semi-retired solicitor) Michael. He had taken a few days off at short-notice because his son was, in his words, in a 'spot of bother'. At the time I wondered whether his son had been arrested by police for a crime of 'moral turpitude', but later learnt it related to his son being stranded somewhere. Good phrase though, I thought: 'spot of bother'. Might use it.

However, Michael later spilled the beans. His son had received a stiff, stern (did he say 'threatening'?) letter asking him to come to the police station to answer some questions about a crime in London. The letter suggested he might be arrested. Michael then went on about how this would involve DNA swabs (as if I didn't know), fingerprinting, all of which was extremely worrying for his son and family.

'He'd have a record,' I added.

'I know,' replied Michael shaking his head in disgust.

I had to bite my tongue about how it might affect his son's ability to travel, apply for jobs et cetera. Michael then went on to express his belief that the police had too much power; powers that should be repealed.

Having discussed the danger and drama of police business for five minutes, he concluded with the words – 'So be warned'. Little did he know what was to happen twenty-seven hours later (I was scheduled to answer bail for an eleventh time).

Well. At least, Michael might prove a little sympathetic, I thought.

Hypersensitivity did not limit itself to tarmac, parsley, traffic lights, but also to the smallest of human interactions, in particular those taking place inside the police station. Although there was a routine to answering bail (fourteen times in total), each was distinct precisely because I was sensitive to every little nuance.

Answering bail for the eleventh time was typical in some ways, but unusual in that it was the longest conversation I had with the investigating officer. Having announced my arrival to the woman at the police counter I took a seat at the far end of the row of grey plastic seats and watched her disappear into the back office. Thinking it was the end-game, I waited. After a few minutes the woman returned to the counter carrying a pad of notes.

I braced myself.

'Sorry, I forgot your name?' she said nonchalantly.

I was not surprised though, the same had happened on the eighth occasion of answering bail too. So much for the police skills of observation, note-taking and reporting, I thought at the time. How many people had gone to jail on the word of this woman? I obliged with my name again and she trundled back into the back office and made a call.

A few minutes passed and the officer returned to inform me that DC Woods was not in office, but a colleague had gone looking for him.

Sigh, I was expected. Sigh. It would seem that DC Woods was in the building. Maybe he was just preparing the interview room.

I intently watched the door beside the reception counter where DC Woods had appeared fourteen months earlier to escort me through the building to interview. I prepared myself to rise to my feet and be escorted through the station once again. I waited. After approximately five minutes DC Woods appeared at the reception counter carrying one page of A4 paper. I was momentarily encouraged, but I noted that on all the other occasions he (or another officer) carried an envelope with the re-bail notice contained therein. Was the paper a re-bail notice? Why no envelope?

I approached the desk.

'Have you moved? You still live at Shrub Lane...?' he asked.

I momentarily racked my brains, what was he after? Were they going to hit me with something else? Was there anything wrong with living in Wantage? (Other than living in Wantage.)

'Shrub Lane is my parents' place. All correspondence can go there. I'm based in Wantage for now, but don't know for how long,' I said thinking that I might have to sell up and move if/when I was charged and found myself without an income.

He said nothing and informed me that I had been re-bailed and handed me the A4 re-bail notice. I quickly scanned the document – re-bailed to five weeks later.

'Your file has been passed the Crown Prosecution Service (CPS) so there will be no more interviews,' he said.

Bizarrely the news didn't spook me out. I was more relieved that an interview wasn't on the cards.

The detective continued: 'They will then determine whether charges should be brought.'

'So what happens then?' I asked.

'You'll be called in and charged if necessary.'

'How long does the CPS assessment take? Weeks? Months?'

'I don't know. So it is possible you could be re-bailed again.'

I wondered how big my file was and how complicated my case. Would it be a priority for the CPS? Was I a priority?

'Because it is with the CPS, that's why it isn't so long,' he said.

I nodded, but I had been here before.

'It has gone on for two years, now,' I said.

'I know,' he replied.

'But that is unusual, isn't it?' I asked. I phrased the question purposefully as I wanted to see how he responded; in the summer of Year 2 he had 'sort of' apologised for the length of the delay – then nearly 18 months. A simple 'yes', would be the easy thing to say.

The detective struggled. I felt he couldn't acknowledge that it had taken, in legalese, 'shed loads of time', but he wasn't able bring himself to say it. No doubt he would blame it all on me though for 'not cooperating'.

'These things take time,' he said. 'Nothing we can do.'

I said nothing. Was there anything to be said? There were words and phrases in my vocabulary: shit, fuck, fuck you, fuck off, for Christ's sake, Jesus. But uttering any of them to the investigating police officer would achieve nothing. Besides I was tired, tired, just too damn tired.

I learnt that if I were to be charged I would appear in court within 7 to 10 days. Presumably a trial would follow within a few months. I wondered what DC Woods was thinking. Did he expect it to go to trial (thereby expecting a guilty verdict)? Was he thinking, I would protest my innocence if I was being wronged?

I took the re-bail notice from him and left by 6.10 p.m. and walked back to the office I had left twenty minutes earlier. The office was just as I had left it, but different – empty but in a strange way, friendly, reassuring. It would be my home for another five or six weeks at least, rather than only 48 hours. If I was charged, I would receive more information (including the 'intelligence' presumably). In the meantime, I was prepared to plod on in ignorance. If there were indeed to be no more interviews, that might not be so bad, I mused. The police couldn't say I had declined to answer certain questions because I had never been asked them. In fact, there had been no questions that had shed light on their logic – why did they think I was the offender when they knew it was a shared house, a shared computer that had not been password-protected nor encrypted?

Y3: 7. Re-bailing Routines Pt 2

Nevertheless, it was a relief that I would not be shown (and questioned over) pictures. I was also pleased that I would not have to go through another routine of answering bail (or so I thought at the time). The act of entering a police station, giving one's name and then waiting for news as one stood at a life-fork in the road, was too draining. Collecting pieces of paper was becoming some of the most dramatic moments of my life. The drama was off-set by the attitude of the police officers manning the reception counter. Sometimes the officers were indifferent and bizarrely inefficient, at other times they were indifferent. Either way, I was never encouraged.

On the eighth occasion (having already been on bail for 525 days) the lady receptionist returned to the inner-office and phoned my details to someone upstairs while appearing to tick my name off on a wall chart. I was expected. I sat and waited. A few minutes later a young man appeared.

'You want DC Woods?' he asked.

The young man wasn't at the door leading into the dark hallows of the station, he was standing behind the reception counter carrying an envelope.

'Yes, I think so,' I said rising to my feet and approaching the reception desk.

He placed the envelope on the reception counter in front of him and said (a little too loudly for my liking albeit to the empty reception area), 'you've been re-bailed again, Mr Anderson.'

I sighed and nodded. Part relief, part resignation. 'Okay.'

'I'm sorry, but we still don't have your equipment, it has been sent away. It is beyond our control.'

'How long?' I asked, fearing two weeks, or maybe a month (which would mean only fourteen days of relief before the nausea returned).

'October 20th', he said, which sounded a long way away to me. He saw me do a quick calculation and helped me out, 'two and a half months'.

'Right,' I replied. 'Is there anything you can tell me?'

'The investigation is still going on. We are now working towards this date as a conclusion'.

I nodded, smiled, sighed and left wondering if my life was all a wind up.

On the twelfth occasion – 752 days on bail (i.e. two years and three weeks; and ten days after my father had been approached by police for a statement) – I introduced myself at the reception counter:

'I have a meeting with Chris Woods.'

'Your name?' replied the burly officer.

'David Anderson. I have a 9.00 a.m. meeting.'

'Yes, I think you're expected.'

It was the first time anybody on the reception counter had knowledge of my visit; something that made the encounter somewhat disconcerting. It was on.

'Take a seat. I'll let him know you are here,' he said.

I kept an eye on the door into the station proper. People, cheerful and chatting, came and went through the door I expected DC Woods to emerge from. After a few minutes, the big, burly desk officer returned. Clasping a brown A5 envelope in front of his midriff, he appeared the most efficient I had met, but he spoke to the foreigners at the other end of reception counter half a dozen yards away and made no move to hand the envelope to them. Although his head was turned in their direction as he addressed them, I detected his body was slightly angled towards me. He then turned his body towards me and moved in my direction while he continued to address the other people's concerns.

155

'Mr Anderson, I have this for you.'

He held out the envelope.

Surely, surely not? Another re-bail? The occasion hadn't even qualified for a charge-rebail probability percentage. I turned the envelope over and found my name and address. I opened it thinking the police couldn't charge me by passing me a bit of paper at a reception counter, could they? Surely there was some sort of formal process? I opened the folded A4 sheet and saw my thirteenth re-bail notice. My eye darted down hunting for the all-important date – always at the end of the paragraph in the middle of the page:

21 April at 3.00 p.m.

I couldn't believe it.

'You've been re-bailed,' the desk officer said helpfully aloud to the station. 'Sorry we can't proceed at this time. It is out of DC Woods' hands.' Again, out loud. In a previous life he might have been a town crier, but no, today, he was a police officer announcing my bail status to anyone who would listen. I thought the case file had been passed to the Crown Prosecution Service? Now what? Were they indeed checking out Mannheim further to my father's comments – 'I think he's been set up'? Apparently DC Woods had asked for Ian's surname but my parents had not been able to recall the names at the time. (Shouldn't be too difficult though, I noted, Ian was on the electoral roll.)

But answering bail was not just about the minutes spent in the police station itself. The whole day had to be built around slipping out of work to answer bail. On the thirteenth occasion (by then 793 days on bail), I had been in a dilemma, did I take a half-day of holiday leave or nip out for a 'late-lunch' at ten minutes to three o'clock? How long did it take to charge someone? Could it be processed in an hour? Sod's law would suggest it would be a long, drawn-out afternoon of re-arrest, interview and charge. That said, I did need to eat something in case proceedings were indeed drawn out over three hours or more. I put off the decision about food hoping the answer would occur to me. Perhaps there would be a telephone call saying don't come in 'today is off'. Or perhaps a phone call from Shrub Lane saying a brown envelope had arrived. But then, out of the blue:

'Do you want pizza?'

'What?'

'It's pizza Thursday, we're ordering pizza. Do you want one?'

The secretarial staff at work were ordering in pizza and so I was able to eat my fill without leaving the building knowing it would sustain me through any criminal proceedings while also allow me to legitimately take a late 'lunchbreak' at 2.50 p.m. and to nip along to the police station.

Having arrived at the police station I endured the ranting of a young man slothfully leaning on the reception desk complaining about something in his life and the police. I informed the officer at the counter and sat quietly at the end of the row of plastic seats waiting for the inner station door to open revealing DC Woods clutching a file waiting to escort me to part two of my life. After a couple of minutes, the same desk officer returned from the inner office carrying nothing but his notepad.

'I'm sorry, who did you want to see?'

'DC Woods,' I said, feeling like an old hand. He disappeared into the back office and I retired again to my seat and sat alone with my shadow.

After a minute or so the officer returned to the counter and looked around the reception area clutching an A5 brown envelope in his hands. That's odd, I thought, he knew where I was sitting. I rose to my feet and approached the counter.

'What's your address sir?'

'Factory Lane,' I replied.

He didn't flinch as he looked down at the envelope. Right, I thought, it must be a false alarm.

'Or maybe Shrub Lane,' I said, surprised to hear a hint of hope in my own voice.

'Right. Okay. DC Woods is not in the station at the moment, but this was left for you,' he said handing me the envelope. I turned it over to see the familiar format.

'Okay. Thanks.'

I walked to the door and opened the envelope. It was indeed another re-bail notice. My eyes skimmed down to the last paragraph where I knew I would find the date. I had been re-bailed to nearly two months later.

Occasionally I was saved from the drama of visiting the station. The day before the ninth occasion was a usual day at the office, but I noticed I wasn't suffering the usual total nausea. Was I again being too complacent or was 'Mr David' tuned into something? Sitting at my desk in the middle of the afternoon my mobile phone rang. Retrieving it from my pocket I saw that it offered no name or number, so I rejected the call. If it was important, I told myself, the caller could leave a message. No message was left. Five minutes later the phone rang again, I rejected the call and left the phone on the desk. A minute of so later, it beeped and alerted me that there was voicemail.

> *Hello this is DC Chris Woods. You are due to answer bail tomorrow at 10.00 a.m.. I am phoning to say you are going to be re-bailed so there is no need for you to attend tomorrow. I will be sending a new bail notice to you. It will probably be about six weeks. Any problems, give me a call on .....*

As the thirteenth re-bail date approached I noted that I would have been on police bail for twenty-six months with nothing to show for it. I wondered if there was a record for being on police bail. Would my (then) 793 days on bail ever be listed somewhere as being a 'missed performance target'? Was someone, somewhere working out the cost not only to the police but to a private citizen (me)? Perhaps it was someone's responsibility to find a way of hiding the missing target or finding a way to brush it under a mat.

My attempts to assign probabilities of outcome were now shot.

According to Chris Woods there would be no interview now that my case file had been passed to the Crown Prosecution Service. Therefore 'interview probability' was 0%, (however, on reflection I give it 1% just in case my father's comments had struck a chord with the detective). I suspected, if the police or Crown Prosecution Service were to discontinue proceedings, I would not be called in. A letter would be forwarded to my solicitor, largely to save face. That left a 99% likelihood of being charged. At which point it became a different ball game.

Yet I had a hope that something would happen. Something that would move my Pickle forward. When I was required to answer bail for the thirteenth time it was around the time of an Easter holiday weekend and a Royal Wedding – an ideal time for the 'next stage', I concluded. If the next stage involved a court appearance the local news, in all likelihood, would be taken up with reports on street parties, face-painting and bunting. There wouldn't be time for reports of proceedings at the local court. But no, I visited the station to find that I had been re-bailed for a further nine weeks until late June, so I had to wait and see if there was anything happening in July that might permit my troubles to be lost to some other newsworthy event. However, I was not satisfied and desperate for a break from the madness I decided to phone DC Woods regarding the possibility of moving the June bail date back to allow me to accommodate a holiday break overseas. DC Woods answered straightaway. Ignorant of the number of cases he had on his desk, I introduced myself with the words 'you're investigating me'.

'I picked up the re-bail notice, thank you,' I continued, feeling sufficiently confident no-one was in earshot as I stood next to the car park adjacent to the empty football court after the lunch-hour.

'Did you turn up?' he asked.

[Course I f*cking did. Jeez.]

'No problem,' I replied, 'I was in town anyway.' [Christ.] 'The reason I'm phoning,' I continued, 'I had thought things would be clarified by now.'

'So did I,' he said.

'Anyway, I'm hoping to get away on holiday. I could do with a break what with everything going on,' I said (not feeling the need to elaborate). I then asked if the re-bail date could be moved back to July to allow me to go away on hiking tours. 'It is approaching two and a half years, so it would be good to get away.'

'Yes, I am prepared to be flexible, if you are. So, if I can call you in to the station if we have news before, then fine.'

'I'm fine with that,' I replied, thinking carefully of my wording, 'but if it takes a turn for the worse, I can still go on holiday? I don't want to spend the money then not go.'

'No, that's fine. You go away on holiday.'

I was relieved and a little surprised that it all went so smoothly. Before we signed off he confessed that he did not know what would happen when I answered bail for a fourteenth time – 'there could be news, or I could be re-bailed again'.

WTF?

Anyway, he seemed fairly cheerful. I was reminded of a news story that judges were more lenient after lunch, when fed and rested. Another note to self: I must get my barrister to wind up his summary statements just before lunch (or immediately after).

Y3: 8. Courtroom Scenarios

My mind often returned to scenarios of me defending myself from the stand. In each scenario I was always referring to Mannheim, her benefit fraud, aggression and scheming but I didn't want to be a one-trick pony. I therefore forced myself to keep an open mind. An open mind would make me nervous, uncertain and, as a consequence I believed, I would (or should) not be completely thrown by surprises. Nevertheless, I worried about acquiring evidence to support my case – the phone calls to the police during the tenancy being one. The calls might have been wiped from the police system by then (four and a half years later) and however well I defended myself in my courtroom scenario, I also knew my head would get scrambled on the stand. I'd get confused, bewildered, smothered by the surreal nature of it all and I would come across as a rambling, incoherent, desperate man on the stand. Holy cow.

My wish to avoid hoping for a particular series of events was reinforced by (and reflected in) my dealings with the Wantage to Oxford bus service. For nine months I had been driving back and forth through heavy traffic to the Park and Ride car park then jumping on a bike for a fifteen-minute journey to the office, however, the bus service stopped only a short walk from my workplace. What bliss it must be, I thought, to stroll up the road from my home, ride a bus to Oxford and be dropped off a short walk from the office. I could read on the bus, browse my iPad and reflect on life as I watched the countryside glide past in the early morning sun. I must try it sometime, I had thought. At least once. And lo and behold, I did. In fact three times in one week. Never again.

A sharp, cold snap in early February froze the VW Golf door-lock mechanism which I took as my cue. I walked up to the town square through the bright morning sun and climbed on to the bus. I waited ten minutes as a bus driver patiently tried to explain to a non-native speaker the company's discount policy for journeying to London over the period of a week. I listened to a young mother yapping away on her telephone only for it to be superseded by the conversation between two young-middle-aged commuters talking absolute f'king nonsense, and I mean pure, absolute, distilled crap. [Apologies.]

The journey back home at the end of the day wasn't great either. It being a cold snap I made sure I reached the bus-stop five minutes early. (Who's heard of a bus that arrives early especially when it had to weave its way through roadworks?) Having waited forty-five minutes in sub-zero temperatures and watched other travellers board other buses, I ran to a larger bus complex just in case I had been waiting at the wrong stop. I hadn't. The bus arrived and I travelled home in disgust as I watched the breath of a thousand, fat commuters drip down the windows of the strip-light-illuminated bus. The second day wasn't much better, but the novelty of travelling with the good people of England was wearing off.

The third day I was not feeling too well, an unhappy combination of a few drinks the previous night, a low appetite (both in the context of a vexed person and a stressed head). As the bus weaved its way up, down and around the country lanes so did my stomach turn, lurch and dip. This would indeed be the last time I would travel by bus, I thought. I readied a plastic bag into which I would vomit in front of a bus full of commuters. I had visions of the bus stopping at my insistence on the country road allowing me to alight and empty the contents my stomach onto the grass verge. After which I would have to suffer the indignity of waving 'thanks' to the mile of backed-up traffic behind the bus (assuming the bus driver hadn't raced off in disgust), mumbling 'sorry' through mouthfuls of mucus and with gastric bile dripping from my lips and return to my seat (the only one available) half-way down the bus next to the woman wearing both an (as yet) unstained, camel cloth coat and a look of horror on her face as she realised the balding, miserable, middle-aged, sicko wasn't going anywhere.

In reality I managed to keep my vomit in check until disembarking a few hundred yards before the last bus stop before work. Frustrated by the bus's slow progress through roadworks, passengers requested the driver open the door. He obliged. Plastic bag in hand, I followed and, spotting two large potted plants framing the doorway of a smart restaurant, I stumbled the dozen steps and retched into one of the pots as a busload of eyes rolled past behind me. So, the moral of the story is the old chestnut – be careful what you wish for. (And take the car.)

There was a part of me that wanted to go to trial. I wanted to see it through, give everyone a good bashing and come out victorious at the other end – a righted wronged man. But in my more tender state-of-minds, my view was: please don't pick on me, leave me alone, you're right, just let me lie down in the corner and die quietly. Sorry for disturbing you. (And: Shouldn't we all be paying the police more for all their hard work which drives them to a fully pensioned retirement at 50 years of age?)

Finally, almost every newspaper crime story had significance. I looked for news of police performance in particular; each led to a new scenario. Reading a report that Manchester Police had started tweeting 'live' from the courtroom, I was aghast. The police had even tweeted about the theft of a bottle of wine saying the public needed to see that justice was being done. On whose terms? I asked myself. Were they tweeting about cases of police brutality, police corruption, incompetence, indifference? And what was 'live'? Was it a commentary during the trial or tweets after a verdict had been delivered? I developed a courtroom scenario based around me spotting a tweeting policeman in the public gallery:

> *'Mr Anderson on trial for downloading indecent images.'*
>
> *'He's looking shifty as DC Woods masterfully outlines the compelling evidence.'*
>
> *'The defence requests information on the intelligence, but the prosecution team is blocking.'*
>
> *'Successfully blocked! Fantastic work by the prosecutor.'*
>
> *'Intelligence is sacred. Vital for ensuring justice. [smiley face]'*
>
> *'Mr Anderson blames it on housemates. LOL.'*

Y3: 9. The Real World

As the years went by something that never diminished was the fear that my predicament would become local (or national) news. I read (and felt for) those who were caught up in media stories. A week before Christmas 2010, a young woman, Joanna Yeates, disappeared on her way home one evening in

Bristol. Her body was found on Christmas morning. The Press spent a reasonable amount of time reporting the story and listing possible suspects. Her landlord, an unmarried, retired teacher, was arrested. The papers ran a profile of him as an eccentric, unmarried, retired teacher and more. The papers were inclined to imply his guilt, but he was released on bail after a few days. I wondered what the police were doing, what they had on him. Perhaps nothing, but he would be forever shaken by the experience, I was sure. Not so much by the arrest itself, but by the media scrutiny.

With no-one in custody, I suspected the police would be feeling the pressure to find the killer of Joanna Yeates. I suddenly had visions of the police knocking on my own front door and arresting me for the murder of the young woman. Somehow, my DNA had been connected to Bristol. I could see the headlines: 'Suspected Paedo held over Bristol murder' and pictures of me with my miserable face being marched from my home by burly policemen just doing their noble job. What would be my response? Any asides to the waiting Press – 'More f*cking sh*t from the coppers'? Or would I actually be chastened, just like I had been on the day of arrest?

After two years, my transformation was complete. I was defined by my troubles. Every breath, literal and metaphorical, was taken as a man on police bail. It was the very fabric of my daily existence. It was brought home to me one Sunday lunchtime when I turned on the television to find an old black-and-white movie with myself in the lead role. (It was, in fact, Henry Fonda but I recognised the man he played as the man I saw everyday in the mirror. I didn't recognise the movie. Having missed the first 15 minutes, I watched as Henry Fonda looked increasingly worried – he was in trouble. I watched more. He'd been arrested, ushered into a police cell, then questioned aggressively for a hold-up at a bank or similar. He looked bewildered but was cooperating and answering questions without the presence of a solicitor. That's a mistake, I thought; I could have told him that.

I hadn't seen the beginning, so I was unsure whether the viewer would know whether he was guilty or innocent. Shell-shocked, he walked from scene to scene in a daze. There would have been a time a few years ago when I would have thought the pacing of the film was far too slow, evidence perhaps of the filmmaker's indulgence. But not now; no, I think, wow, they've nailed it. I suspect that those viewers who have experienced similar things would appreciate the pacing.

Henry Fonda's character was charged, bailed and court proceedings instigated. He struggled to find witnesses who could have proved that he could not have been the person who had committed the crime – witnesses had died, others moved away. His wife became increasingly anguished and was eventually committed to a hospital for mental illness.

Henry Fonda's character was formally identified by witnesses (cash tellers) and underwent two trials (the first being a mis-trial). Anyway, he was innocent. Separately, the police arrested a man for a hold-up of a shop and the lead detective noted the physical resemblance to Henry Fonda's character. The man was identified as the thief by the same cash tellers who had identified Fonda. All charges against Fonda were dropped. The film ended with his wife being released from hospital a few years later and the credits reported that they had eventually moved to Florida. The end credits also stated the movie, *The Wrong Man*, was based on a true story.

There were other reminders of the life I was leading. Channel-hopping one weekend I found myself watching an American documentary on a small-town-America criminal case. The documentary included reconstructions and interviews with a woman (a victim of an attack), her husband (investigated and charged with the attack) and the investigating police officers.

The woman had worked as an administrator in her local church. Her husband dropped by the church one lunchtime and then left (at a time when a silver-haired man was seen loitering by the church). The woman was attacked with a hammer and funds were stolen from the church. She survived the attack but her head injuries meant that she was unable to remember details of the attack. The documentary reconstructed how the police arrested the husband and didn't follow up the lead of a fingerprint of a local suspect because they discovered the husband had his lover (and even her son) to stay in the marital home while his wife was recovering in hospital. The documentary reported how the husband was questioned without a lawyer present and the police starting framing his replies to suit their plans.

The documentary appeared to present events as a miscarriage of justice as they interviewed those involved and described the various courtroom trials. I watched and waited for the denouement – the release and castigation of the police of their failure to follow various other leads. Slowly the programme ran on and concluded with the report that the husband had been jailed for the attempted murder of his wife. Though still unable to recall the incident, the wife was a minute away from testifying in support of her husband at his retrial, but, on account of her medication being changed 24 hours before she was due to take the stand, she had become confused and had run from the courthouse.

The documentary's interviews concluded with footage of the healthy-looking husband, but the head-and-shoulder talking-head shots had not quite revealed the setting of the interviews until the end – a whitewashed brick room with wire-meshed windows – a prison! I had been watching a story (empathising

167

with the husband as the authorities built a case against him) to find that he had been in prison for twenty years.

Heading to bed that night and relieving myself I looked down at the swirling event in the toilet bowl and struggled to disassociate it from my own life. Not that I could complain. Much worse was happening to many, many others – events beyond their control blighting their lives. How much is a person their 'own person' if they are not permitted to be their own person by the exercise of their own free will? What proportion of the planet's population could be described as being their 'own person'? If 'free will' was the greatest gift to humankind, then was the denial of that gift the greatest injustice of humankind?

Finally, on another occasion, I caught part of a documentary on Strangeways prison. The documentary profiled one 42 year old man (a year older than me) who was in jail awaiting sentencing for a drugs smuggling conviction. He seemed a decent sort. He was hoping for a light sentence (even a non-custodial sentence) so that he could get to see his eighteen-month-old child grow up. I channel-hopped and returned to the documentary for the conclusion. He appeared stunned. He was in shock, he said. He had been given fifteen years (having been advised that he might expect eight years at worst). He would be in his late-fifties before it was all over.

Y3: 10. Defence Preparation

I did not have to rely on television programmes to remind me of my predicament. There was always the post. In Year 3, I received the standard letter from my solicitors Blacker McCann listing bail arrangements, but the date the letter said I was required to answer bail was incorrect (by one day). I phoned Blacker McCann advising them that the date needed to be corrected, but it worried me that the solicitors were making little errors. I had concerns about the errors and omissions of the police, but if my legal team were dropping a ball or two, that was a cause for concern. Enclosed with the letter was a leaflet on Legal Aid which set out the conditions and costs for defendants. At first glance I noted two things: I would not qualify for Legal Aid support and, secondly, that the solicitors charged £200 per hour for representation. It brought home the seriousness and the expense of the next stage. (And why were the solicitors sending this to me now? My status had not changed in two years. What did they know that I didn't?) On second reading, it appeared the limitation to Legal Aid funds was for the Magistrate's Courts only. My case would be upgraded to Crown Court (for the more serious criminal) so I should be Legal Aid-supported. Yay!

In the late spring my solicitor Alex Watt returned my various calls and we spoke for the first time in about a year and I felt perfectly justified in expressing my frustration with the police delays. He said that he had spoken to DC Woods who reported that the detective was also frustrated 'with the CPS' and the delay. Apparently the CPS wanted more investigation. I asked Alex, 'isn't there a time limit?'

'Not on the serious cases. i.e. those that go to the Crown Court. If a sentence is less than six months, then the case must be processed within six months. Crown Court cases can take as long as they want.'

I explained to Alex that one concern that I had was that as time went by it was more difficult for me to account for my whereabouts on any given day. I had moved house twice, had left one job before becoming 'self-employed' for 15 months only to start another office job in a new institution. Furthermore, the boss in my original job (at the time in question) had moved posts into semi-retirement, a former co-worker had left her job, married and emigrated, another office-sharing work colleague had changed jobs, got pregnant and given birth.

'Well, we'll just have to find them,' he said.

What? Fly Mel back from Asia? Who would pay for that? Moreover, how did one broach the subject in the first place? How on earth were my former colleagues going to remember events (of irrelevance to them) dating back four years?

I spoke of the former co-tenant Mannheim and how I hoped to review the police file and, if appropriate, follow it up with legal action against her. Alex assumed I was talking about criminal charges, but I was really thinking about a civil case. The standard of proof in a criminal case might be too high.

But before that happened I knew that I might face a grilling as a defendant in my own case and therefore should be prepared. I felt I ought to write down all my imagined responses and propose possible cross-examination strategies my barrister might wish to use to undermine the testimonies of Linklee and Mannheim – scenarios of Mannheim being picked apart to a point where she exploded on the stand doing half my job for me in front of the jury. I worried that I ought to follow up the leads on the credit agencies and the City Council who had been chasing Mannheim and Linklee. Would that be something the solicitor did? Perhaps with the services of a professional investigator? There was no mention of it on the information slip. If I provided details of everything to the solicitor would they then submit a variety of requests to the court getting all the information on my phone calls to the police, the credit agencies, background checks and more? Perhaps Mannheim and Linklee had been screwing other people around and I could establish a pattern of behaviour, I wondered.

But, once again, my imagination was not always about courtrooms, it was about being exposed as a man awaiting trial.

As I drove home from the garage reflecting on my disappointment that I could not justify an upgrade to an Audi (and having also endured a few days of illness, no doubt from tiredness and underlying stress) I was suddenly aware I was going to be sick. I was one mile (two minutes) from home and believed I could make it in time. Thirty seconds later I realised that I would not make it home before I threw up. I considered my options. In moving traffic I was too slow to manoeuvre into an upcoming lay-by. My options limited in the next fifty yards I had a sudden image of myself being sick in the car: I would reach home with the dashboard dripping with the contents of my stomach only to be too tired and unwell to clean it up before collapsing sick into bed for the night. As I would be too ill to move the following day, the bile would stew in the warm May sun. Neighbours would soon call the police due to the strange aroma coming from my car leading to the local police learning my identity and about my troubles. Data Protection requests from residents would lead to the release of further information and, before you know it, the headline in the local newspaper would be 'Vomiting Paedo in Our Midst'.

All this flashed through my head as my stomach churned and traffic pushed me through a residential area. Fortunately, I spied a driveway entering a public-looking building, but seeing another driveway into some sort of establishment with pleasant grass verges, I drove on. F*ck, it was a secondary school and the kids were emerging ('Vomiting Paedo Caught in School-Grounds'). I swung onto the verge on the main road on the other side of the road from the school, stumbled out of the door and, clutching my rear car bumper, hurled onto the beautiful grass as cars rolled by. No one stopped. I concluded that perhaps I was better without a car thus avoiding the possibility of newspaper headlines altogether.

Y3: 11. The Distractions

In the spring of Year 3 my Sydney-based brother visited the UK with his family (wife and two boys). He had witnessed a particularly difficult time during his previous visit six months earlier (twenty months into my bail period). My composure had crumpled, so he had suspected something was not quite right. However, on this occasion I attended a few dinners and chatted away happily. I was invited to Australia and once again I nodded and agreed that it sounded exciting while I screwed up my forehead in thought and muttered a phrase along the lines: 'Yeah, don't quite know what I will be doing this summer.'

That said, I had been eyeing up a three-week tour in China. Ultimately these distractions were attempts to move me away from the deliberation of courtroom scenarios and helped me gain some perspective. At times I wondered that if my edginess was a plant, enough could be harvested from the fields of Thames Valley to feed the planet. Whatever, I was keenly aware that courtroom scenarios were a waste of time. Similarly, I didn't want to keep focusing on a German woman. In fact, I was fast reaching a point where I did not care whether I won or lost any court case, I just wanted to be shot of the craziness in my head and I was in no doubt that my predicament was damaging my heart muscle.

Otherwise, it was DVDs and movies that provided the daily distraction. I worked my way through seven series of *The West Wing* (for a second time) spending hours with CJ, Josh, Toby and POTUS. The opening theme tune was a balm to the soul in itself and I knew I had 45 minutes of peace and non-judgemental company.

I spent an evening watching the film *2012* about the end of the world; two hours of earthquakes, landslides, volcanoes (showering the world in burning rocks), super-heated pyroclastic flows and finally mountain-size tsunamis. I wish.

The film's director should try making a movie about two years on bail, I found myself thinking as the credits rolled. It might be beyond him.

I worked my way through the TV mini-series *Band of Brothers* – ten episodes following the 101st Airborne Division through the Second World War. As I slumped on my sofa munching my way through crisps and downing gin and tonics it almost got me wishing that I could be part of something big and life-defining (at which point I realised that was precisely where I was).

Running, martial arts and squash helped to burn through some of the nervous tension. A few gins and tonic and a few glasses of wine also helped relax me, but I was ultimately disappointed that my life had been reduced to carefully managed self-medication: box-sets, exercise and alcohol. As I reflected on such matters, my mind inevitably turned to a German living far, far away. There was a lot to answer for.

Y3: 12. China

[Reader, once again a chapter on a holiday break. Feel free to skip this chapter.]

Eventually the summer arrived and, having checked in with the police station, I left the UK in late June and spent nineteen days on the other side of the planet. China was a fine place in which to lose and refresh oneself. A different language, culture, ancient civilisation. I landed in Hong Kong and took a taxi to the tour hotel and met the perfectly pleasant Chinese tour leader, Mike. The group of fourteen was made up of a Canadian couple, two Australia couples, two Australian friends, a Norwegian, a Brit, an American and a mother-daughter combo from Australia. From Hong Kong we headed to Guangzhou to swelter in humidity as we walked around a park before climbing onto an overnight train to Guillin and then a bus to picturesque Yangshou. After a tour of the city we spent a few days wandering around the countryside (littered with the impressive limestone karsks formed at the bottom of a sea 150 million years ago), indulged in a spot of cormorant fishing in the evening before heading off on a day trip up the River Li. Returning to Guillin we boarded a train to Wuhan, then a bus to Yichang where we boarded a cruise boat for a three-day river trip on the Yangtze River.

The days on the river were spent leisurely reading, visiting the Three Gorges Dam Project, drifting through various gorges and chatting with group members and tour guides including Ava, a river tour guide based in Yichang. Ava recited poetry, gave me little history lessons and showed me the tea ceremony. With promises to keep in touch and host Ava's visit to the UK, the tour group disembarked the boat and headed to Chongqing, a massive city (municipality) the existence of which I had been wholly ignorant. I suspected none of its thirty million residents would ever hear of my troubles, whatever the outcome.

From Chongqing we headed to Chengdu, saw some pandas and explored parts of Wenshu. Under overcast skies we queued to see the Great Buddha at Leshan. An overnight train took us to Xi'an where we visited a pagoda, took a calligraphy class before visiting the museum and flea market (where I bought a scroll and a painting for my home). The following day we boarded a private bus to visit the terracotta warriors excavation site, stopping off at a clay modelling factory on the way. The excavation site (with museum) was truly remarkable and I was fortunate to get my guidebook to the archaeological site signed by the discoverer of the site, eighty year old Mr Yang.

An overnight train from Xi'an brought us into a hot and humid Beijing. Exhausted after many days travelling (including limited sleep on overnight trains) and the heat of the enormously busy city, Mike led the tour group to Tiananmen Square, Mao's Mausoleum and the Forbidden City on our first day. Early the following morning we headed by bus to the Great Wall of China in the Huairu District of Beijing. The physical exertion of a morning on the wall (including a walk to tower 23) was not the problem, rather the heat and humidity of the Chinese summer. Later that day we visited the Pearl Market, the Temple of Heaven monument and various other gardens.

The following day the tour formally ended, but not before a visit to the Summer Palace. After a few goodbyes to my friends at a forgotten metro station, I moved to another hotel in eastern Beijing for a few days. After a visit to the Lama Temple and the workers stadium I found myself at the Sanlitun Yaxiu Market. I spent most of my time on the third floor of the massive clothing centre looking at suits and haggling down the cost for a tailor-made, light pin-stripe suit. I placed an order and bought some ties before resting some tummy trouble on my final day.

I gave some thought to the Pickle, but the trip helped put matters into perspective. Some courtroom scenarios played out in my mind – all completely useless. Nothing would resemble the reality, I knew. I wouldn't be so bright, brilliant and calm on the day, I was sure. Bizarrely (mostly in Beijing), I passed (and exchanged glances with) a few individuals who could have been a Chinese relation of DC Woods – similar facial features, proportions, deportment and manner. I always found myself being a little bit more accommodating during any interaction. Perhaps the presence of the detective, and everything he represented, had seeped in my subconscious. I was unable to read anything into the tarmac of Chinese roads (though the state of some of them was pretty shocking).

On the final day I rose and soon realised that I would miss my flight from Beijing to Dubai. At the airport, I managed to arrange a midnight flight to Dubai, from which it would be easier to board a flight to London. I realised that I ought to alert my parents and, with the assistance of helpful staff at the information desks, I accessed my email accounts from their back offices (Internet was only available once travellers had passed through security). I opened an email from my mother which read: 'Your next appointment at the police station is at 4.00 p.m. on Friday (this Friday 15th). Hope you get this ...'

Typical. The first time I had ever missed a flight (of my own doing) it was the day I was to be charged with an offence which would make the hardest criminals wince. I could only assume it was unhappy news. I was confused that I was being required to answer bail within seven working hours of my landing at Heathrow. (My letter to DC Chris Woods before my departure had said: I would 'return the evening of [Thursday] 14th'.)

I wondered whether my delayed return would be used against me. I emailed my mother explaining that I had missed the flight and was trying to make new arrangements and asking her to inform DC Woods and my solicitor. Funnily enough I was not too troubled regarding the imminent bail date. My stomach did not plummet.

Y3: 13. UK

I arrived back at my parents in Oxford in the middle of the afternoon on Saturday 16 July. There was the usual chit-chat about the holiday but I detected their concern about the police matters. I picked up the two messages left by DC Woods asking me to call him on my return which prompted some concern in me too. Never before had there been a request to get in touch with him (and with some urgency). Something had happened. Too tired to call that day, I deferred it to the following day – Sunday. As I departed my parents' home for my own home, I prepared my mother for an unhappy development.

'It is probably because they are going to charge.'

My mother looked confused, concerned. 'Why?'

'What else are they going to do? Why else would they be following up for the first time in two and a half years?'

'But had you seen those pictures?' asked my mother.

'No, the police interview was the first time,' I sighed.

'I think it is Ian,' my mother said, decided.

'No, I think it is her,' I replied quietly.

'Why?'

'I just do.'

I didn't want to get into a long explanation about Anna T. Mannheim and the computer dialogue boxes. It was the one thing I could not prove. Besides, if my mother were to be called as a defence witness, then she shouldn't blurt it out only to have a prosecutor take her to task about some of the details.

'I had been expecting something was going to happen,' I said, hoping that would be the end of it. 'I went to the police during my shared tenancy about my concerns.'

I realised it was the first time I had mentioned my interaction with the police during the Meadow Road tenancy with Mannheim and Linklee. Sharing the tribulations of everyday house-sharing was not something I had ever done. That said, both my parents were aware of some difficulties I had had at the time (and had even been called upon to witness the departure of Mannheim and Linklee from the house, such were my concerns). My mother did not know it, but it was something to which she might have to bear witness to one day from the witness stand.

'Do you have a record of the calls?' she asked.

'No, but the police should have them,' I replied (on, what I hoped was, the well-placed assumption that all phone calls had been recorded).

'Will they have them after all this time?'

'I don't know,' I sighed. 'We'll see.'

I was quite relaxed. Or was it tiredness? Or resignation? It had been a long haul and there was no suggestion that it was going to slow down. I was aware I had to pace myself.

It was not the first time my mother had asked me if I had seen (i.e. been responsible for downloading) the images. The first time had occurred nine months earlier. I had dropped by their home and as I made a cup of tea I explained that the police would probably follow through with a charge (based on DC Woods' words in a phone conversation before I was re-bailed for a tenth time).

'How many pictures did they find?' my mother had asked.

'They showed me twenty-two.'

'And was it you?' she asked quite nonchalantly.

And there it was, I had noted at the time. The poison had taken hold.

I had stated my position having emerged from the police interview (a year earlier), but apparently, that was not enough. I could not help but think it was a 'result' for Mannheim. It had taken nearly twenty-two months but the German had finally managed to sow doubt between family members.

'No,' I had said, tired.

In fairness, it was to be expected and I had no doubt that more 'results' for Mannheim would begin to pile up.

Y3: 14. Answering Bail no. 14

I called DC Chris Woods at 1.30 p.m. on the Sunday and left a message on his voicemail. The phone rang at 2.30 p.m. as I unpacked my rucksack. I sat on the edge of the bed, amidst the unwashed clothes and handful of souvenirs from China, and answered the call. We greeted each other and he immediately asked me to come into the police station, 'today if possible'. I had mixed feelings, it was a forty-minute drive there and forty minutes back. It was Sunday and I was still jet-lagged. That said, I was half-minded to travel in that day to avoid any complications with my working week. A big work conference was scheduled off-site on Wednesday and Thursday and getting out of the office might be problematic. I wondered if the months since April had produced something the police wanted to quiz me on. Perhaps they had actually been interviewing Linklee and Mannheim. Did I have the strength to do battle with Mannheim's machinations that day? Not really, I concluded, before DC Woods dropped the bomb.

'You're going to be charged,' he said.

There was a slight turn of my insides, but not too much. I leant back on the bed, settled into the cushions and took a breath.

'Do I need a solicitor there?'

'You don't need to, but it is your right to have one present, but it would take longer because you'd be put in a cell until a solicitor is available unless you could coincide your arrival visit with Alex.'

'Is Alex on call today?'

'I don't know.'

We agreed that I would phone Alex and then call the detective back.

As a rule I didn't like calling people on their mobile phones on a Sunday, but I felt there were sufficient grounds for concern that day. Alex answered immediately. I apologised for the call and explained that DC Woods had asked me to come into police station without delay to be charged. Alex was genuinely surprised and reported that DC Woods hadn't intimated to him that I was going to be charged. I was surprised that Alex Watt was surprised. It was even reassuring to know that I was not the only one behind the curve.

I reported the exchange I had had with DC Woods about whether I needed a solicitor present or not. Alex confirmed that there was no need for a solicitor for the charging itself, but he was more than happy to arrange for someone to be there with me.

'It is completely procedural,' he said.

Still bathing in my restful holiday state, I was not fussed whether a solicitor was present or not and I certainly didn't want to spoil someone's Sunday afternoon. We talked through the next steps which would include a court appearance in ten to twenty days' time.

'I expect that you would be pleading 'not guilty'?' Alex added carefully.

It was difficult. In my professional (and general) life experience I could not recall anyone accusing me directly or indirectly of lying or being untruthful. When it does happen it is surreal, unnerving, depressing. It is one of the qualities of civilised, polite, compassionate human interaction that there is a presumption of truthfulness especially when it is one-on-one. Not that Alex was contesting my previous statements, but it felt as though he was checking.

'Yes,' I replied, reiterating that the deleted images shown to me in the police interview room had been new to me.

'And you think it was your housemates? The German girlfriend?'

I explained to Alex that I didn't want to publicly accuse anybody (although, of course, I did think she was responsible), but I could confirm that I had had considerable difficulty with the housemates and had had three conversations with the police at the time ahead of anticipated trouble.

I was pleased that Alex remembered the German girlfriend (or rather 'girlfiend' as I was increasingly inclined to describe her). He must have read the document I had forwarded to him over 18 months before.

'One concern I have,' I said, 'is whether those conversations with the police will be available?'

'I don't really have the answer,' Alex said. He had not asked the police for the (phone call) recordings before because he had not wanted to give them the opportunity to suppress the evidence, he said.

I paused and processed his words.

'What do you mean? Why would they do that?' I asked. Before he had a chance to respond, I continued, 'If they're after "truth and justice" then it is in the police's interests to make them available.'

Alex snorted with laughter. 'They're not interested in that,' he said. 'They have targets.'

I was taken aback. I had read in the news media that the police had targets, but, having been brought up to respect the police, to hear a legal professional (whose judgement I broadly trusted) speak with such disregard of those with whom he had daily contact was very depressing.

(I later recalled that I had raised the matter of police targets myself with Alex Watt after the first re-bailing. He hadn't reacted at the time and I had felt a little ashamed to insinuate such things.)

We talked further about the police in general. He was not too complimentary about the majority of officers describing them as untrustworthy. I asked about my case officer DC Chris Woods, whereupon Alex reported that he would place the detective in the top fifty per cent of trustworthy officers.

'Fifty per cent?!' I exclaimed.

'Top thirty per cent,' he corrected himself. 'I have always found him to be courteous with prisoners, the accused. Whereas DC Lauren Hopkins, your arresting officer – you'd be a notch on her career post. Don't be fooled by the blonde hair and pretty looks.'

I did find it a little difficult to believe the (alleged) ruthlessness of DC Hopkins. Though no one should be blamed for being fooled by blonde hair and pretty looks, I certainly wasn't fooled (that said, she did look nice and had pretty hair).

In all seriousness, I liked to think I was not as stupid as I looked or sounded. Alex wouldn't detect it down the other end of the phone, but I felt a little indignation rise in me – DC Hopkins could have a go, but she might find I was not the pushover she thought I was.

Alex and I talked about the need to complete Legal Aid application forms and I confirmed that I was happy to endure the charging procedure by myself.

After the call I scribbled notes of the discussion and made a mental note to purchase a Dictaphone to record the thoughts that would come tumbling into my head now that matters had escalated. I phoned my parents and was quite matter-of-fact about reporting the developments. I then phoned DC Woods and confirmed that I was coming in, but asked if I could drop into Sainsbury's first, 'The house is empty of food and Sainsbury's close at 5.00 p.m.'.

'Yes, fine,' he said.

I asked him if I could park near the station thinking he might invite me into the station car park knowing that I was being so helpful coming in at short notice, but no.

'You could risk parking in by the station, but the wardens are particularly fierce and efficient in the area.'

Was I right in thinking a police officer was saying I should consider committing a parking offence? I was tempted to voice my interpretation of his advice, but thought better of it.

Later that afternoon I entered the police station in casual gear – knee-length shorts, a plain T-shirt, body warmer and comfy trainers. No thought was given to how I looked. It was not about impressions this time. Little thought was also given to the contents of my small shoulder bag – spectacles, notebook, pen and a bottle of water. My routine on the previous thirteen occasions had been completely different – there had been great care in the selection of the clothing and a visit to M&S lavatory. There was no long walk down from the town centre – this time I approached from the other direction. Everything was different. All the visions of my 'last moments' of a man with no police record were inaccurate and inconsequential. All that time spent dreaming up scenarios was wasted. A total waste of energy. I made a 'note to self': try to banish all incoming scenarios for future meetings, events, occasions and just let everything wash over me.

On arrival, I was pretty relaxed – the result of three weeks in China. It had distracted me, relaxed me and given me perspective. These 'troubles', I estimated, would swallow up eighteen months of my life (in addition to the twenty-nine it had already swallowed up). If the case went to court by Christmas and there was an unhappy conclusion, I might spend (according to my research) twelve months in jail, whereupon I would emerge for the next phase of my life (albeit with, dare I say, limited options).

My trip to China had helped bring perspective to the fore – a global and historical perspective. Global: I was one person on a planet of seven billion, each with his or her own story of trial and tribulation. Historical perspective: in 247 BC the first emperor of China, Emperor Qin, was making arrangements for his death and burial. To escort and protect him in his journey into the after-life he intended to have 8,000 soldiers buried alive with him. His prime minister managed to persuade him to have the soldiers made of clay rather than be buried alive. Every one of the 8,000 Terracotta warriors of Qi'in had been based upon an actual soldier; every clay warrior was different. All those soldiers escaped an early pointless death, but their existence was immortalised. And so would my own tribulations and trial recede into the abyss, ultimately to have no relevance in any meaningful way. I wondered whether I would have felt this way if I had not had three weeks in China. The jet lag probably helped a bit too.

I entered the reception area at 5.50 p.m. There were a few people present, but it felt quiet, restful. I passed on my details to the reception counter officer and took a seat at the end of the row where I had sat on numerous occasions with a quivering tummy. This time I was cool and calm. I noted that one of the three reception counter staff members was the officer who had told me during my tenancy that there was nothing the police could do at that time about Mannheim unless I made a formal complaint.

At 6.00 p.m. the door opened and DC Chris Woods appeared. He scanned reception, but I was sure he had no trouble remembering me. I rose to my feet and joined him at the door leading into the station.

'How are you?' I asked quite chummily.

'I'm fine, thanks.'

'Sorry about Friday,' I said as we headed along the corridor towards the back courtyard.

'No problem,' he said lightly, 'you don't want to travel back from China when you're ill.'

'Yeah,' I said, nodding.

How did he know I was in China? My pre-departure letter to him had never listed my destination. Perhaps it had been fed back to him via my parents and solicitor; still, it was unsettling.

We arrived in the courtyard behind the station where, 18 months earlier in the darkness of a December evening we had waited as his colleagues had booked in other 'prisoners'. There was no wait this time and travelled swiftly up to the custody desk. On the way, to make casual conversation (and to avoid awkward silences), I asked him when my charging would be in the public domain.

'Will I find it in the newspapers at some point?' I said. 'I need to start telling a few people.'

'I certainly won't pass your details to the Press, but, of course, after a court appearance it might be reported.'

I noted he referred to the first person 'I', in some way making it clear that *he* would not pass details to the Press. I believed him. However, I wondered if his police colleagues might tip off the Press as a matter of routine (and for a small fee?). Such things were the talk of the moment – the *News of the World* phone-hacking scandal being headline news.

The custody desk area was quiet and, there being no custody officer available to book me in, DC Woods showed me to a waiting room. The room had no handle to the door, no lock, no free-standing furniture, just a built-in bench and table-top. He stood at the door, propping it open with his foot while he kept an eye on the custody desk waiting for an opportunity to book me in. I say 'book', I mean 'charge with a criminal offence'.

I slung the small shoulder bag from my shoulder, unzipped it and removed a bottle of water. I unscrewed the top and took a swig.

'Don't let the others see that. You not supposed take drink in here.'

'It's only water,' I said.

'I know, but there are some people who come in here and drink things they shouldn't. I know you're not, but some would. When you are in the station you are under our care.'

It was all quite chummy.

Moments later at the custody counter, we began with a series of familiar questions: 'What job do you do? Do you have any injuries? Are you on medication? Feeling suicidal?'

I sighed inwardly.

'I think I'm okay today, thanks,' I replied leaning on the counter.

I had been last asked that question over a year and a half earlier (before the second police interview); a different time, a different response. I had no idea what was going on, my film and livelihood having walked out the door. On this occasion I wondered what DC Woods was thinking. He had been present on that occasion and had not confiscated the memory sticks. Whether that decision was informed by my protest, I didn't know.

'Do you want a solicitor present?' asked the officer. 'You have your rights.'

I turned to DC Woods. 'There is no need, this is procedural,' he said.

This concurred with Alex Watt's words, so I was happy.

'I'm okay,' I said, nodding and reflecting on the civility of the whole process.

The charge itself appeared on the screen embedded in the counter. DC Woods read it out which I assumed to be the formal process of being charged. I moved towards the screen to see the wording for myself.

> *Make indecent photograph / pseudo-photograph*
> *of a child*
> *Between 02/01/2006 and 17/02/2009 at Oxford in*
> *the County of Oxfordshire made indecent*
> *photographs, namely 560 images recovered from*
> *unallocated clusters from exhibit LPM/9.*
> *CONTRARY TO SECTIONS 1(1)(A) AND 6 OF*
> *THE PROTECTION OF CHILDREN ACT 1978.*
> ... ...

I noted that it was 'make' rather than 'possess'. I was aware it was the formal legal term. I had looked up the difference in meaning between the two in the months after my arrest, but had long forgotten the definitions. The dates seemed to be very broad – a three-year period. It was the first time I had come across them. The 17 February was the day of arrest and there was no reason to suspect something was going on the day before the visit by the police. I had been playing squash the night before and had then gone to bed. The 2 January date didn't apply to anything as far as I could recall. Did something happen on 2 January 2006? Why three years? I could only conclude it was a block of time because the date-stamps on the deleted images had been lost.

There was only one device – the Apple tower. There was no reference to hard-drives, DVDs, CDs, the Apple Powerbook. I had a hazy memory of the 'unallocated clusters' phrase (or something similar) from the second police interview. 560 images. A high number in some ways, but not in others. If one webpage had, say, a hundred images, then they could be downloaded in moments in a three year period? I was not sure whether to be concerned or relieved.

'Only one charge,' said DC Woods. Again, I didn't know whether this was good news. Could there have been more? At least I knew what I was dealing with. After two and a half years, it was something. Since there was no mention of the Apple MacBook Pro I considered asking for its return, but decided to leave that to another day.

I had anticipated being charged as the most traumatic experience of the whole ordeal, but I remained relaxed. Also, it being six o'clock on a Sunday evening, there was no one else in the custody counter area, so it was not as embarrassing as it might have been.

I was handed a printout of the charge after which the custody officer worked on allocating me a court date. I was asked for my address. Well I have two, I thought to myself. I turned to Chris Woods for help.

'Where do you live?' he asked.

'Well, Wantage,' I replied, 'but I might not be there for long.'

I hoped I was making myself clear to him – I might lose my job meaning I couldn't make mortgage payments on the house and would be obliged to sell (most probably at a loss).

'Your work?' asked the custody officer. I sighed. (I did not really want to give the details of my employer.) I had always considered that which generates an income as 'work', however, on this occasion I was inclined to keep my salary-provider out of it.

'Two things,' I sighed out loud. 'I am sort of self-employed, but not earning yet.' Then I mumbled something about doing a bit of administration hoping it was vague enough. I didn't want to lie; it wouldn't help my case.

My answer was tapped into the computer. It seemed to do the job.

'So what happens now?' I asked. 'I understand I receive a file on the case?'

'Yes, before the appearance at court a preliminary evidential file will be passed to your solicitor. Statements et cetera.'

Preliminary? There would be more? But I did not take it further. I wondered whether it would include the 'intelligence' and witness statements by former housemates Linklee and his girlfriend, Mannheim.

I was handed the re-bail notice and noted the date of the appearance at the Magistrate's Court two and a half weeks away. I wound up the discussion with DC Woods and he showed me to the exit. As I strolled back to the car I, once again, noted that it was different to the way I had imagined it. In all the scenarios of the infamous day of charging I had imagined I would be walking the other way up the road. And I was calm, not in the dazed, vexed state of my imagined scenarios (though I knew there would be much more pacing and fretting in the months ahead). What I did have was a clear appreciation that 'life' was now just something that happened *to* me, I was a spectator, not an actor. It was something to be endured, or, on a more positive note, I just needed to find a way to live through the drama. After all, it was all of part of life's rich tapestry, as Joseph Campbell would say.

I headed straight home, grabbed a Chinese takeaway and sat and watched Yimou Zhang's *Hero* – a little bit more escapist China. As the day drew to a close I stood looking at the pots and plates in the sink and reflected that they really did now belong to a man charged with a criminal offence. It was going to be an eventful and difficult week. A challenging rest-of-the-year. After nearly two and a half years, phase two of this miserable business had begun.

Year Three (Y3): July

Y3: July: 1. Briefings, Work
Y3: July: 2. Briefings, Family
Y3: July: 3 The Fall Out
Y3: July: 4 Briefings, Men
Y3: July: 5. Briefings, Women
Y3: July: 6. The End of the Beginning

Y3: July: 1. Briefings, Work

Now that my Pickle was official (and in the public domain) the time had come for friends, family and work colleagues to be briefed. I could not delay sharing the news until my first appearance at the Magistrate's Court two weeks later. But, in the meantime, I needed to equip 'an office' to kick-start preparations for an eventual trial. I browsed the Internet for a Dictaphone, a small laser printer and a scanner. There were combined laser printers and scanners, but I had to think about my cash-flow – there was a very real possibility I would not have had an income by the end of the week. That said, I was soon indulging in a little bit of shopping therapy on the basis that I also needed some distractions. So, in addition to a laser printer and a scanner, I ordered a DVD box-set of a television sitcom and a few DVDs. The movie *Avatar* was suitably escapist and it had echoes of my own storyline: a creature (feeling blue) fights a bunch of baddies whom he once thought were allies. With no access to space-age technology to fight the good fight, the creature had nothing but his own sense of right and wrong, belief in destiny and, finally, a flying dragon (the one thing I was missing in Wantage) to fight his corner.

With regard to my employer and work colleagues, I intended to leave breaking the news until Thursday at the earliest – my workplace was running a two-day conference on Tuesday and Wednesday of that week and there was no point in rocking the boat until the event was over. My first day back in the office, Monday, passed without incident. No-one would have noticed anything different about me.

Thursday arrived and I prepared myself for a long day. I decided to raise my Pickle with the head of the department that day, if not, the following day (Friday) allowing him to mull it over at the weekend. I checked his diary with his secretaries trying to find a slot. I needn't have worried, for at about 10.00 a.m. he invited me into the office to discuss the restructuring of the department that would result in greater responsibility for me.

He sat behind the large oak desk with me on the other side, notepad in hand. He appeared relaxed, possibly relieved that the conference had concluded satisfactorily. On my part there was mild anxiety and resignation about where the conversation would eventually lead. During the twenty-minute talk he invited my opinion on his plans. I responded as best I could knowing that the words that would fall from my lips a matter of minutes later would change everything. His plans were redundant.

The discussion slowly moved to a conclusion and he started to adjust himself in his chair in an indication that the meeting was coming to an end. I sighed. My time, two and a half years in the making, had come. I jumped in.

'There is one thing I want to put on your radar which may affect matters,' I said quietly. 'I have some difficulty in my personal life which may impact the department's work in due course.'

I had his attention.

And I started.

'I am involved in some legal difficulties which have been going on for a few years but they are about to take a turn.'

I explained that I was contesting the allegations and then described the police visit, my time on bail, the criminal charge itself and my shared housing arrangements at the time of the alleged offence. He appeared reserved, even lost for words. I concluded my report within two minutes. Thoughts of my involvement in the reorganisation of the department were a distant memory for both of us. He wished me well and stated that they would be supportive and the information was confidential. I explained that I intended to have similar conversations with three other members of senior management. We rose from our seats. He looked mildly shocked as he stiffly walked over to his computer and I left the room. One down, albeit the most difficult one.

I walked straight to the office of the second-in-command, Charles, and asked if we could speak.

'Sure,' he replied.

I closed the door (which I could see puzzled him) and sat. My composure wobbled slightly at one point in the five-minute explanation, but otherwise I held a true course. Charles was a man of the world and had been in the middle of a number of challenging situations in his professional life, so I was confident that he had seen stuff like this before; he did not appear ruffled.

Then it was Michael Bull, the in-house solicitor responsible for personnel. His office was next to mine and much of our business overlapped. We were regularly in and out of each other's offices. I put my head around his door and I asked to speak to him. He obliged and I stepped inside. I could detect that he could detect that I was troubled. As I sat I noted that it was ironic that I had often been in his office rolling my eyes at the predicaments in which staff had found themselves. Now, here I was, his buddy and partner in employment about to land a whole heap of rubbish in his lap.

Distracted by a lot of noise coming from the world outside, I requested that he close the window by his desk. He obliged without batting an eye, but I was aware he knew this was fast becoming an unusual meeting.

I ran through the basics (past living arrangements; police visit; bail, charge), wobbling only momentarily. I explained that there was a court appearance scheduled two weeks later after which my case would be in the public domain. I expressed my wish to inform my work colleagues myself rather than they read it in a newspaper or hear it on the grapevine. Michael was solid and kind, though I was aware he would be thinking of the employer-employee ramifications. We finished within ten minutes.

I was exhausted and it was only lunchtime. I took a ten-minute stroll through the rain to the gym in order to renew my annual membership knowing that I might not qualify for a discount through a workplace scheme in the not-too-distant future.

After a few vexed hours of waiting, I met the remaining senior staff member. As I concluded my explanation he asked what it had to do with him which threw me; I explained that employers usually felt obliged to take a position on such things. As the meeting ended and I rose to leave, he somewhat unusually walked around his desk and offered an outstretched hand. We shook hands and he wished me well.

His office opened on to the (public) reception area. I was aware that my cheeks were flushed and my eyes welling up, so I kept my gaze down as I passed the receptionist (someone I line-managed) to the security door round the corner. As I was about to reach out with my swipe card the door was 'buzzed open' by the receptionist leading me to the conclusion that she had seen my troubled state and taken pity on me. It was proving to be a long day indeed.

I left the office building soon afterwards and headed to the gym to work off the tension. Seeing an old work colleague and friend, Owen, playing football nearby, I thought about suggesting a drink and sharing my news. Owen needed to know because he might have to be called as a defence witness at a criminal trial, but no, I decided to leave it to the following week. The day had been long enough.

I had always felt the real psychological hurdle would be informing my employers rather than breaking the news to siblings (which could be left to my mother), so, with the first challenge accomplished, I phoned my mother from the cycle-park and explained that it was time to sweep up the rest; she was free to update my three older brothers and one younger sister. My mother could provide a relatively objective view and it would allow my siblings to digest the news without putting them on the spot. I certainly didn't want to have four identical conversations and I could follow up with further details and arguments in the following days.

I climbed on my bike in the failing evening light and started the forty-minute journey home. 'So here we go,' I mused; two and a half years of waiting and now it all begins.

Y3: July: 2. Briefings, Family

Later that evening at home I could not summon the strength to do any creative work so I settled down to some DVD distraction during which I received a text from my brother, Joe:

> *Hi D., M has told me what you have been going through and I am shocked. How you have managed to stay sane is COMPLETELY beyond me. But that is a testament to you. Give me a call if you want to chat and I will call you back. Let us meet tomorrow or during the w/e. Come and stay the night and unwind if you like. God D. You are a brick and have the total love and support of the family. But you know that, I know.*

You don't know Joe, but if you did you know him, you would know that life was getting weird. At the best of times he would struggle to write 'best wishes' on a birthday card. Obviously my news had had an impact. I acknowledged the text saying I would be in touch.

The following day, Friday, was a quiet day at work. I did not see the departmental head (which was probably no accident), however, I did the see the in-house solicitor Michael to say 'hello' making sure everything was normal (outwardly) while my (inner) piglet squealed. Mid-morning I received a text from my eldest brother Anthony who worked as an Independent Financial Advisor and was a rare texter:

> *David we all behind you supporting you. Let me*
> *know if I can help in anyway. Anthony.*

I acknowledged it and thanked him. Shortly afterwards I received a text from my little sister Maria, mother to five young kids, and husband, Sebastian.

> *We are deeply shocked by what you have gone*
> *through. We want you to know we are 100%*
> *behind you. You WILL get through this, and we'll*
> *help you every step of the way. We love you lots.*
> *We are here when you need to talk. Maria and*
> *Seb x*

Again, I acknowledged and thanked them for the text.

I received a phone call from the Blacker McCann solicitors who had been hand-holding me since the day of my arrest. They wanted to talk about Legal Aid among other things. I was not able to talk in the office and said I would call them later (while quietly thanking God for living in a time of mobile phones). Having found a quiet street at lunchtime, I returned the call from my solicitor's office and spoke to Raquel.

'I just want to check one thing. You earn £45,000?' she asked.

'Approximately,' I replied.

'Then, I'm afraid, you will not be eligible for Legal Aid. Anybody earning over £22,000 is not eligible.'

'But I may lose my job in a matter of days.'

'Well, then you could apply for Legal Aid,' she said matter-of-factly.

Oh that's a relief. Not all bad then.

Raquel soon started talking about their rates for representation – £180 per hour (plus VAT). I enquired about the solicitor's time required for my first court appearance and the bill I should expect for that one appearance.

'About £300.'

F*ck that, I thought.

'Can I represent myself?' I asked.

Not that I was being serious, but I was agitated that I had to pay three hundred quid to deal with a situation which, as far as I was concerned, was someone else's mess.

'Do I have to have a solicitor present?'

'No, you are perfectly entitled to represent yourself.'

Not that I would, I thought (and mumbled).

I expressed my desire to have a meeting with my assigned solicitor before my appearance in court. I wanted to lay out my case and get started on my defence. They knew little about me and I knew next to nothing about the legal process ahead. Perhaps sensing my unease at the cost of the court appearance Raquel told me that there was no need to meet the solicitor before the court hearing.

Um, I was unsure.

She confirmed that I was obliged to pay for the Magistrate's Court stages, but should my case go to Crown court (as expected), then I would qualify for Legal Aid support.

I asked about what would happen at the court.

'You should arrive at 9.15 a.m.. Your solicitor will be given a dossier listing the main evidence against you. You will be able to consult your solicitor and review the dossier in a side room before heading into the court to make a plea.'

'How long will the whole process take?'

'Difficult to say. You may be in court at 3.00 p.m.'

Another day's holiday leave gone, no more breaks for me (my remaining eight days of holiday leave would be consumed by solicitors and trial rubbish). As the call concluded I confirmed that I did indeed want a solicitor present at the hearing. I also realised that all my conversations now seemed to be about matters relating to my legal status.

I received a text from my brother Andrew in Australia:

> *So sorry to hear what you have been going*
> *through over the last two and a half years.*
> *Thinking of you and let me know if I can do*
> *anything. A. et all.*

I spent an evening with my brother Joe in a town centre pub followed by a restaurant. Interrupted by a few quiet mild wobbles of composure I ran through events (and my frustrations of fourteen re-bailings) over the previous two and a half years. I shared my theory that Mannheim was involved. Joe had known the woman and the troubles I had had with her; there was the possibility that he might also be called to appear at a trial. He was amazed that I had kept my troubles to myself saying it was something he could never have done in the circumstances and would blab about it from day one. We agreed that such was the difference between brothers. Nevertheless, it was good to talk about the whole matter after all this time and to receive a level-headed, supportive response to my troubles.

And following up his text I received a voicemail from my brother Anthony.

> *Just to say if you ever want to talk, I am around all day tomorrow. Very sorry to hear all the nightmare you're in the middle of; I just, you know, feel so much for you. So anything I can do just let me know. If you need to chat, want to chat, give me a call, matey. OK. Speak soon.*

Wanting a whole day away from explaining myself, I left it twenty-four hours, until Sunday. When we spoke he asked how things were going and whether the solicitors were any good. I explained that I was happy (though had nothing to compare it to) and there was no reason to look elsewhere for the time being. Like Michael (my solicitor work colleague), Anthony believed that it was wise to press for a meeting with the solicitors ahead of the court appearance and come up with a strategy. He even offered to call the solicitor on my behalf. Anthony had had difficulties with an ex-wife for years and had been in and out of the courts so the world of legal-wrangling wasn't new to him. I had heard reports of his pacing about the house as the strains of the breakdown of marriage took their toll. I referred to his experience in the courtroom, but he said it was nothing compared to what I was facing (though I was inclined to differ – give me the police any day).

During our discussions of the legal state-of-play I had been quite calm and methodological in my replies, but when Anthony asked how I was holding up, my composure started to crumble. With the phone pressed against my ear, I stood in the kitchen pinching my nose as I focussed hard on holding my emotions in check. Silence rumbled on for twenty long seconds as I fought to control my breathing. I aborted a few attempts at starting a sentence.

'Take your time,' he said realising what was going on at the other end of the phone.

I eventually regained my composure and we continued. I gave a broad summary of the situation and the previous two and a half years. I thanked him for his offer to come down to support me in court, but I explained that the upcoming hearings were purely administrative, so there was no need. (I did not share that I was also motivated by a desire not to contaminate family life with court business.)

In the bathroom after the call I splashed water on my face and caught sight of a dark purple mark running across the bridge of my nose. On closer inspection I realised that it was a bruise created as I had pinched myself during the telephone call. I surprised myself at the ferocity of the pinch but, I noted, life would be full of little surprises from now on.

Finally, a few hours later, I spoke with my baby sister Maria (aged 39 with five kids of her own). In contrast to Anthony's conversation, there was very little discussion about solicitors and, in some ways, the call with Maria was the most difficult for me. Talking about the very nature of the criminal charge was laced with angst and despair. Like anybody else, I was all too aware of the 'no smoke without fire' reaction. That said, Maria was steadfast in her support. I explained that I was happy to accept the heat for the time being, but all I ask was that people reserved judgment.

It was times like this that I became angry with the (suspected) architect of all this misery for whom the strain on familial relationships was, no doubt, all part of the plan. I hoped there would come a time when I could smash the record straight.

Over the previous few days my explanation had taken the form of three simple observations, the first two of which were statements of fact. The third was, I hoped, a deduction from the first two statements. Rather than people request that they 'believe me' (which I thought complicated and placed a burden on the listener in the circumstances), they were invited to acknowledge this trinity of observations. The first observation was: I was contesting the charge (a fact that did not require support or belief). The second was: the suspect (me) was not a stupid person. (I took a liberty here that I hoped would be broadly acceptable to those who knew to me.) The final observation was deduced from the first two: he (me) was contesting it, he was not stupid, therefore he must have his reasons and his defence a logical basis (grounds for contesting the charge).

On Sunday evening (one week after the criminal charge), I rested in the knowledge that all the family (and my immediate circle) had now been informed. The world had changed. It was a matter of letting events play out. That evening, as I watched the movie *Terminator 3* for possibly the third time, one line uttered by the T1000 struck me: 'Anger is more useful than despair'. I nodded to myself. I must work on my anger, I thought. Nurture it, love it, develop it.

Y3: July: 3. The Fall-Out

Returning to the office on the second working day after breaking the news to my employers, I felt that I had already done the hard work. This second week (as a criminal suspect) was about dealing with the fall-out. I was soon told by the boss's secretary that my weekly 10.30 a.m. meeting with him had been cancelled – apparently there was a special departmental management meeting (between, it so happened, the four colleagues whom I briefed the previous week). Holy cow.

Fortunately though, the secretary told me, she could re-arrange my meeting for 3.00 p.m. that afternoon.

Okay, I thanked her.

I watched my office neighbour Michael Bull (responsible for personnel matters) from the office next door shoot off to the meeting at 10.30 a.m. It was a meeting about me, I concluded. That was the only explanation. It was ironic that my weekly meeting had been hijacked to discuss me and my predicament. Perhaps the termination of my employment. The department could not have someone in their workforce who had been charged with such an offence. It would have been the first time that I had been fired. And this wasn't a matter of being fired from a bar-tending job or unskilled work. No, this was being fired from a middle management, white-collar position. It left a mark.

I tried to get some work done, but it was difficult. I watched the clock. They were still in the meeting room down the corridor over eighty minutes later. Aware that good news travels fast, my insides sank. They were thrashing out how I was to be 'let go'. I imagined a discussion as a few colleagues were supportive and sympathetic to my position and wished for me to remain in post, but there would be a few longer-term members of the organisation who saw the reputation of the organisation as paramount and, no doubt with regret, all threats to the reputation must be dealt with promptly and efficiently.

At 12.15 p.m. (105 minutes after his departure), Michael returned to his office and closed his door (which was unusual in the 'open door' work environment). I concluded that he must have been getting down to the business of processing the paperwork for dismissal. A colleague nipped into my office for a quick chat to update me on the filing of documents on a new filing system. I nodded attentively as he spoke (as if I could give a fig about document filing) while watching Michael's door. As my colleague and I talked, I saw Michael open his door and pop his head out looking towards my office before retreating inside and closing his door again. My colleague wouldn't have noticed that, as he prattled on about filing protocols, my own head wasn't in the discussion.

A few minutes later I was left alone in my office again with only expletives and expressions of disbelief swirling about in my head; all the while I sat at my desk patiently and quietly 'working'. I'd have looked no different to the seven hundred-plus days I had already worked there. At 12.25 p.m. Michael's door opened; he popped, nay, 'leaned' into my office and, with a concerned professional look on his face, uttered the words: 'can we talk this afternoon?'

My stomach, heart, anything that could sink, did. (Sink or plummet? It all felt the same nowadays.)

'Do you want to do it now?' I said helpfully and politely. Let's get it over with now and be done with it, was my only thought.

'No,' he replied, 'I have a few things I need to do right now.'

Okay, I nodded. Right.

'Two-thirty okay?' he asked.

'Yep, fine. Great.'

He 'leaned out' and returned to his office. Holy, holy, cow. I had been clearing up my desktop, files and emails since my talk with the boss, but the reality of imminent dismissal was shocking.

I continued to work as best I could, but I was unable to focus. I imagined the conversation that afternoon and the various scenarios. I would be upright and dignified and understanding and there would be no fuss. I knew Michael had

had three conversations terminating employment during the previous four months. One was a woman who had been made redundant after about five years of employment. When the news was broken to her, she left in tears and shock. Another thirty-something who had been here on a short-term contract was let go at short notice (more tears of disbelief), and another fifty-something chap (who had been recently going through a divorce and had been employed on a twelve month contract with a view to an extension) was 'let go' after nine months and given four working hours (18 hours in total) to wrap things up and leave. Brutal. I knew Michael didn't like doing such things and had not expected to be involved in personnel matters when he had arrived twelve months earlier with other duties, nevertheless, he was fast becoming an old hand at sacking people (at the boss's behest). I wouldn't make it difficult for him.

I reviewed my immediate work diary that had a meeting with a visitor scheduled for the following day, so I called one of my team who agreed she would make herself available to see the visitor if I were unavailable. (I didn't give my reasons.)

Unable to concentrate, I left for an early lunch and headed to the gym to de-stress and work through the fired-and-departure scenarios. Did I say goodbye to people or would Michael prefer that I slipped away quietly? I hadn't expected it so soon. I thought there might have been a few weeks to work things through. After all, it was eleven days until the first appearance in court and my name and charge reached the public domain. My employers were under no obligation to make a decision before then, surely?

I kept turning over the length of the management meeting that morning – one hour and forty-five minutes. Looking at my reflection in the mirror as I rowed, I reached the decision that I would 'insist' on explaining my departure to work colleagues.

Michael might not have liked the idea thinking that I might have bad-mouthed the institution, but I had no intention of doing so. If necessary I would have invited him to join me in the briefings as I looked people in the eye and ran through the 'trinity of observations'.

Despairing as I watched my pale features fight the blotchy flush of exercise, it occurred to me why 2.30 p.m. had been proposed for the meeting with Michael – he finished work at 3.30 p.m.; he would need twenty minutes for the chat-of-termination, then thirty minutes to wrap up the paperwork as I made my way out of the building. It matched the dismissal routine of at least two of recently fired employees. I also noted that the boss had to catch a train at 3.00 p.m. that afternoon, therefore he would slip out of the building at 2.30 p.m. just as I would be going into the meeting with Michael. Everybody's day had been all planned around me being issued with my marching orders.

The fast-working pistons of my imagination tired me out. After all, being fired was the least of my worries. It was just one part of a bigger, more gruesome picture, but at least it would clarify matters. It was not as if I would have missed the place. However, there were matters regarding my own house. Would I have been able to get help to cover the mortgage? Or would I have to sell the house straightaway? Then, of course, there was the small matter of the criminal trial.

I returned late to the office after my extended lunch-break. Who would care?

Through his open door I saw Michael sitting at his desk.

Did I go in early and get it over with? Or did I struggle on for twenty minutes and allow their plan to go through smoothly? Let the boss get his train while I was being fired and let Michael escape at his designated time?

I felt pretty much physically sick as I tried to kill the twenty minutes, tidying emails and my desk. At 2.15 p.m. Melanie, one of the boss's secretaries entered and casually mentioned that the 3.00 p.m. meeting with the departmental boss proposed earlier in the day would not be taking place as he was heading to London.

Yep, I know, I said. Thanks.

It was clear Melanie knew nothing.

'But,' she continued, 'the boss has asked to have the meeting tomorrow morning.'

What?

What did she know that I didn't? Was she just innocently and inadvertently reporting a brush-off from the boss when she had brought to his attention that he would miss my re-scheduled meeting if he was heading to London.

'Oh, we'll meet tomorrow,' he might have said, knowing full well I wouldn't have been in the building.

I was confused. Unless I was being let go later in the week?

I explained to Melanie that we would sort it out later that afternoon after my 2.30 p.m. meeting with Michael.

Two-thirty p.m. arrived and I slipped into Michael's office, closed the door and sat. Michael seemed his usual professional self.

'Well, we had a meeting this morning.'

'I guessed,' I said nodding philosophically.

'And there are three options.'

Okay, I said.

'Firstly, dismissal, which, I have to say everybody around the table rejected as an option. We are not going to go there.'

What, I think? I'm not going to be fired?

'Secondly, carry on as we are,' he continued. 'Or the third option is to invite you to consider applying for 'Special Leave' on full pay.'

Wow. I turned over the idea in my head, checked and re-checked the suggestion. I would be 'on leave' and be paid? It seemed like a slam-dunk. What was the catch?

'I thought I was going to be fired,' I muttered. 'I guessed you were in a meeting this morning that's why I asked if you wanted to meet before lunch to get it out of the way.'

'Yes, I realised when I was at lunch that you might have jumped to that conclusion. Sorry.'

Michael and I talked more. I expressed surprise. The plan seemed generous (and I said so) considering what I had been expecting. (And, of course, regardless of what I had been expecting.)

'It serves both our interests,' Michael explained. 'It shows we've done something. It allows you time to work on your case.'

'I thought I was going to be fired,' I repeated.

'Everybody around the table was of the same mind that the first option was not on the table. Besides, if we had let you go you could have us over the barrel of a gun at a tribunal about pre-judging your case.'

'But I wouldn't do that,' I explained. And I wouldn't have done. My troubles had nothing to do with my employer and I understood the predicament that they had found themselves in.

'No, I know you wouldn't, but still it is a consideration.'

The spinning of my world gradually slowed and the tightness in my chest, head and limbs began to loosen. My breathing had remained constant, but my inner-being eased as it inhaled the fresh air of knowledge, where previously I had been gasping in ignorance.

'You don't have to make a decision now,' Michael said. 'Sleep on it and we'll talk in the morning.'

'Okay, but I think it will be a 'yes'. Don't you?'

Michael nodded. I was still a little disorientated, but I didn't think I could see a catch.

I shared my wish to tell others in the building – to look them in the eye and explain the situation and the reasons for my 'absence'. Michael reported that senior management wanted to keep the matter entirely confidential as far as possible, but he would check with colleagues and get back to me. My insides sagged as we talked about legal and court procedures but, like that flash of light as the sun sinks below the horizon, I realised that not only would my special leave allow me to get stuck into trial preparation, it might also allow me a bit of time to be creative. Perhaps it was not all bad. I shared my thoughts on a trial as we wound up the meeting. I didn't have the fight in me yet, and said as much to Michael, 'I feel pretty beaten up'. But I now had time to regain my strength. I wondered to what degree my 'survival' would require me to find a way to embrace events for to 'stand up to them' just looked too exhausting.

Later, I reflected on Michael's reference to words attributed to John Lennon: 'life' is what happens to you when you are busy making plans. Although pertinent to a degree, I realised that I hadn't really made any plans for two and a half years.

Y3: July: 4. Briefings, Men

The following morning Michael popped his head round the door.

'Still okay? Still yes?' he asked referring to our discussion the previous day.

'Yes,' I replied. 'Is there any reason why I shouldn't?'

'No,' he said with a nod and smile before disappearing.

I usually attended a 9.15 a.m. management meeting, but I was unsure whether I was welcome now that I had caused all this trouble and would soon be away for a few months. Five minutes before the meeting I popped my head round the boss's door.

'You want me at the 9.15 a.m.?' I asked pleasantly and professionally (I hope).

'Yes, he replied, without missing a beat almost surprised as if 'why not?'

Why not? Because, as far as some people were concerned I was a crazy paedo, I thought with a sigh.

Okay, I smiled cheerfully and professionally (I hoped). There is always a tension between the workings of the mind and the workings of the world, but at times like this, it was more of a battle of opposing forces.

I was still waiting for clarification about who else in the workplace I could tell, but it did not delay the briefings of others outside my work and family circle – friends and sports colleagues. Mid-week I started with my karate club (at the first session I had attended since my return from China). I entered the dojo to a few chummy 'welcome backs', before being caught by the man I had wanted to update before any others.

'Are your three week holidays longer than everybody else's?' sensei Luis quipped, good humouredly.

'Er, yeah sorry' I replied, intending to update him with my news in the relatively confidential environment of an empty changing room after the session.

'You coming on Sunday?' Luis asked. 'We have a presentation of certificates.'

'Um, I don't know. Er, maybe.'

Plans take a back-seat when defending oneself against a criminal charge; I couldn't think that far ahead, besides, the

Sunday in question was five days before the court appearance and I had wanted to get my head down and prepare a briefing paper for the solicitor. So, on reflection, no, in fact I hadn't been planning on attending.

After the session ended two hours later, I headed to the changing rooms and was soon joined by Luis. I casually asked that if he had a few minutes to spare I wanted to update him on something.

So, amidst towelling and talcum powder, I began by saying that I was involved in a legal dispute. Explaining that I was contesting it, I swiftly moved on to the meat of the matter. He was, as expected, solid and understanding and could not believe that it had been going on for two and a half years and spoke of a work colleague who had experienced a similar situation (images on a computer) that, Luis said, had been eventually attributed to a malicious co-worker. I was fairly philosophical and chatted around it. I left it to him to advise club members as he saw fit, however, I said, I would like a word with them subsequently to provide further detail. The only slight wobble of composure was when we parted and he offered his support and opportunities to chat 'whenever'.

Owen and I had shared an office ten years earlier after which we had met up every other month to have a beer and a bite to eat. In fact, he had had a walk-on part in the film confiscated by the police. He was solid, stable and undramatic and we shared the same dry sense of humour. We had spoken earlier in the week about scheduling a drink because, as I had told him, I had 'some news'. He had subsequently emailed me saying a football friend of his might want to join us, but he had sensed from my phone call that my news might be confidential. I called him and said that, yes, the news was confidential, so we agreed to meet for lunch alone. And so, on a beautiful July day

I cycled to a favourite cafe, ordered brunch and selected a table out of earshot of other diners. Owen joined me ten minutes later. We wrapped up the small talk in less than fifty seconds. And then my news.

I used the same tried and tested format of delivery: legal difficulty; contesting it; then details – arrested, bail for 2.5 years, criminal charge, appearing in court the following week.

I described the place from where my inner comfort came and referred to the difficulties I had had in the Meadow Road property. I invited him to consider the trinity of observations and reserve judgment.

Owen was both taken aback and supportive. We talked through some of the legalities and challenges of my situation. I explained I was mentioning the matter to a few people because it would enter the public domain imminently. If a few sympathetic persons in my circle were aware of my Pickle, then they could act as a conduit for information to a wider circle (which might include former work colleagues, acquaintances-once-removed and others).

'So, if it comes up,' Owen asked, 'I can say you spoke to me before the story broke and I say 'he didn't do it'?'

'No, no,' I replied, genuinely alarmed, almost surprising myself. I realised that I wanted people to be critical, doubtful. I didn't want people to feel obliged to accept my side of the story. I just wanted them to reserve judgment. 'Just refer to the trinity,' I continued. 'He's contesting it; he's not stupid; he's contesting it with good reason.'

'Okay,' he nodded. 'Okay, yeah right.'

Owen noted that I must have had a difficult few years.

'Well, it's been interesting,' I reflected aloud. 'I've learnt that a man, can be hormonal.'

Owen looked at me quizzically, half-thinking I was being funny but I was being deadly serious.

'Sometimes I have been fine when events were challenging – for instance, when I was charged ten days ago I was fairly cool and philosophical. But there have been difficult periods, sometimes for no reason.'

It was at this point in the conversation that I wobbled. I paused to regain my composure. That was another lesson I was learning. When recounting the facts of the case I was methodical, calm and objective. It was when the listener enquired after my emotional, psychological state that I got blind-sided by, er, 'weakness'. Any reference to the emotional turmoil I must be experiencing, slapped me hard across the face just as I was about to deny its existence or treat it as just another fact of being on bail for criminal charge of a sexual nature. It was almost as if the inner-weakness was lurking in the shadows waiting for me, nay, even daring me, to deny, its existence. I concluded that the reference to the turmoil forced me back to reflect upon the thousands of hours spent pacing around the house; the days where I would be driving to and from Oxford only to see the dual carriageway blur as eyes welled up and obscured my vision. Or the times when I would find myself in the corner of a darkening room running through courtroom scenarios and waiting for the next stage of the legal process to kick off.

As this realisation turned over in my head I let my gaze fall away from Owen's face to the sausage and baked beans on the plate in front of me, possibly themselves cooling towards me.

I was conscious of the dozen people sitting about us in the cafe. To an independent observer I would look like someone in distress. This compounded my embarrassment as I suddenly didn't want the diners to jump to the conclusion that Owen and I were 'breaking up'.

Owen and I chatted more and I explained the phone calls to the police and other possible evidence I had in my armoury, but I also withheld other information; it would all come out in due course. Besides, I didn't want to fight my battle here. As I had said to Anthony on the phone at the weekend, I just wanted to wage war once – in the courtroom. It was too exhausting otherwise – fifty 'effing conversations.

Before we parted he offered support – not only drinks in the coming weeks and months to alleviate the stress, but also money for the legal fight. I was surprised, touched and flattered, but declined the kind offer explaining that I did not want to be financially indebted to him.

'Well, you would be,' he laughed.

I eventually received clearance to talk to work colleagues about my difficulties and my imminent 'special leave'. Quite by chance, I saw the Building and IT Managers alone in their shared office at lunchtime. I popped my head around the door and asked if they were both around later. No, not necessarily, came the replies, so I closed the door and began.

'I have some news. I'm taking some special leave. I may be away for a while.'

Okay, they seemed to nod indicating a wholesale lack of interest.

Having explained that management wished to keep the matter confidential, I ran through a summary of the difficulties in my personal life (not private, because it might not be private for long if the local newspapers were sniffing around).

Neither colleague blinked. Perhaps they were too taken aback. I continued.

I explained that on the day of arrest I asked about the nature of the intelligence received. The police said they were not going to tell me and to this day they had not told me what it was. I described the repeated re-bailings over the years, which, I had been told, was a good sign – my case was not a priority. Furthermore, the police might be struggling to establish what had happened (as reported by the investigating officer to my parents earlier in the year).

'I returned from China ten days ago to be charged with one offence (two years, five months to the day after the arrest).'

I sighed and paused.

'Although I am deeply unsettled, unnerved by the whole situation, I am, on one level, sort of comfortable (as comfortable as one can be in the situation) as it is not entirely unexpected for reasons I'll explain in a minute.

'I reported the situation to senior management last week. There has been discussion over recent days, because, understandably, employers are obliged to take a view on such matters. It has been agreed that I take special leave to sort this out. And so I may be away for a few months.

'I am telling you this because I want to avoid the rumour mill in the weeks and months to come. You will now understand the nature of my absence and can plan accordingly. Furthermore, it may move into the public domain in due course and I wanted you to hear it from me and not read something in the local paper.'

I concluded with a few details of the defence – the shared house, the unprotected computer, the difficulties with housemates that had led me to seek advice from various quarters at the time – and said I was hopeful that colleagues would reserve judgment. It was embarrassing and humiliating, but there you go.

That pretty much concluded the five-minute explanation. Both colleagues nodded and took it all in. The IT Manager said he would pray for me. The Building Manager looked like he was dying for a cigarette.

I did not know if I was unconsciously playing it easy – I had briefed Luis, Owen and the Building and IT Managers – all men. I was aware my alleged crime was a man's crime. Men might listen to my story and think 'there but for the grace of God go I', but a woman? My story might just confirm her misgivings about me or men in general. Or, perhaps, she might know the type of person I had been dealing with during my years in Meadow Road. Anyway, the time had come.

Y3: July: 5. Briefings, Women

I line-managed two women (Sarah and Sara both aged about 30) and worked very closely with a team of three women secretaries. I purposefully identified the afternoon of my penultimate day (before my 'special leave') to have my talks with them. I needed them to sleep on the news and then interact with me for at least seven hours to demonstrate that all was well and that things could operate normally.

I slipped into Sarah's and Sara's office and casually suggested we head to a small social room with comfy armchairs and a quiet atmosphere for a quick chat. Knowing that suggesting such a meeting (and venue) was unusual, I put them ease explaining that there was not a problem with their work.

Settling onto a sofa opposite Sarah and Sara I cut the small talk and calmly explained that I was taking (prolonged) leave from the workplace and I wanted to explain the reasons to those colleagues with whom I worked most closely.

'I am in a legal dispute and I am taking some time away from work to resolve it,' I said, beginning my monologue.

I filled the minutes with talk with very little discernible reaction from the ladies opposite, but, all credit to me, there were no wobbles. The conversation (monologue) goes on a little longer than usual possibly because we were all comfortable in the comfy seats unlike the 'conversation' with the boys that morning when I was casually leaning against a filing cabinet shifting from foot to foot.

There were a few questions after I finished but no discernible shock. We agreed to have meetings the following day in order to handover.

My head spinning ('this is crazy') I returned to my office. My solicitor colleague Michael dropped by fifteen minutes later, closed the door and took a seat. Even though we had had adjacent offices during the twelve months we had worked together, it was the first time Michael had actually sat down in my office.

'I'm off now, but I just wanted to wish you luck.'

(He wouldn't be working the following day, Friday, my last day.)

'Just to let you know I have emailed your home contact details to myself, so if you don't mind I may call you in the coming weeks to see how you are.'

'Sure,' I said, 'thank you.'

'And if you are unhappy with the representation you are getting, get in touch and I could speak with former colleagues who may be able to recommend other solicitors.'

'Okay, thanks. That's very kind, but it seems to be going okay,' I replied. 'I have been speaking to my brother who has had some difficulty in the past going through an unpleasant divorce and he suggests I have a strategy before I appear in court a week tomorrow. So I am going to insist on seeing a solicitor at the firm.'

'Yes, that's good. Although it is just another day for them, they should understand that this is a very important process for you. Tell them you are a complete novice at this and you want some peace of mind. It's money well spent.'

'Yeah,' I sighed, nodding.

'Chin up and have faith in yourself,' Michael said buoyantly (as convincingly as a solicitor could).

Yes, I thought to myself. I needed to have faith in myself just as I had done when I was shown the handful of images in the police interview eighteen months before. I must have faith in my initial reaction, I told myself, which was all very well but I sometimes did catch myself thinking – had I gone crazy? Was there some parallel existence in my psychology? Was I in some form of denial? But such thoughts did not last. I always returned to my gut reaction on seeing the images. I trusted my instinct. I had known at the time that Mannheim was up to something and I thanked my lucky stars that I had made a record of the difficulties with her.

Michael and I rose to our feet and shook hands. I thanked him.

Finally, time for possibly the most difficult briefing – the three secretaries on my floor. Early twenty-something Hala (recently) from Pakistan; twenty-five year old Danielle, and finally relative new-comer (of five months) forty-something Melanie. Having waited until they were all present together, I joined them in their shared office and closed the door smashing a filing cabinet as I did so.

'Don't do that, be careful. This is an important filing cabinet, full of important material,' Danielle teased me. 'You must treat it with absolute care.'

I sighed inwardly, little did she know what I was about to explain to her in the coming minutes. Closing the door to the office in a workplace with an open-door policy did not go unnoticed.

'Are we in trouble?' chirped up Hala enthusiastically.

'No.'

'Are *you* in trouble?' Danielle chirped up enthusiastically.

I sighed again. F@ck.

'Sort of.'

'What have you done?' someone chirped up enthusiastically.

I took the remaining seat and sat with them around me in a square circle.

'I'm taking some leave and I want to explain why,' I began.

The talk went relatively smoothly and I covered all the ground. I noticed Danielle's shock and even blushes when I mentioned the police visit and my arrest, at which point, I had their absolute attention. Up to that point, there had been a slight joviality and 'what's all this about then?' sense to the discussion. Not now. I had a captive audience. As I spoke I met their gaze, occasionally looking away 'at the horizon', as I worked my way through the story. I faltered and wobbled as I explained there had been difficult times and that this whole process of informing friends, family and colleagues was embarrassing and humiliating.

There was one pause in my monologue of ten to fifteen seconds as I sat head down gazing at my knee trying to compose myself, trying to deliver the next words without my voice breaking, all the while feeling a tear thundering slowly down my right cheek. Glancing up once I saw a tear rolling down the stunned expression on Danielle's face. Silence – an aberration in a place usually buzzing with chatter between three lady-friends. I could feel all their eyes on me and in a way noted the peculiarity of the situation, a middle-ranking member of the management team explaining to (junior) colleagues the humbling, socially and legally perilous situation in which he had found himself.

Having finished, I invited questions and tried to encourage some lightness to creep into proceedings. I explained that it was the police's right not to disclose information even though it had been two and a half years. I answered a few more questions as the usual mood of lightness started to push the dark shadows aside. The discussion came to a close after approximately twenty minutes. I was unsure what tomorrow, my last day in the office, would bring. Would there be awkwardness? If there was, there was nothing I could do about it.

I returned to my office totally whacked. No more for today, I thought.

There were a few more people to tell, but I left it to the following day. I slipped away unnoticed, avoiding a 5.00 p.m. social event (ice-cream tasting). Those in the know would understand why – tired, exhausted, embarrassed perhaps. I headed home and had a wholly unproductive evening.

Y3: July: 6. The End of the Beginning

Soon after arriving in the office the following day (my last before I started my 'special leave'), my line manager, Charles, entered my office breezily.

'Look, I'm in London for most of today and I just wanted to say good luck,' he said warmly.

'Thanks.' I replied, shaking his offered hand.

'It's a tough situation, God, and I hope it all works out.'

During the morning I met with Sarah, Sara and Hala (all of whom I had briefed the previous day) regarding work matters to be handed over. They had had a chance to sleep on the news and all seemed fine, with no hint of awkwardness. Before lunch I brought three other colleagues together and delivered the spiel. The academic was a little embarrassed (but I was unsure whether he was embarrassed on my behalf), the clerical assistant seemed surprised at the news (but, being the youngest of the three, he probably had limited experience of life's rubbish) and the man from finance was pleasantly supportive saying he hoped I came through it intact.

In the last hours on Friday afternoon I had a short handover meeting with Hala, the young twenty-something secretary recently arrived from Pakistan. As the meeting concluded she tentatively asked what would happen to me. I explained it could be resolved happily (and I returned to work) or unhappily and I ended up in jail. I might get a suspended sentence.

'Is that when you buy yourself out?' she asked quietly.

I paused, squinted and processed the question.

'Can you do that? Give someone some money?' she whispered.

'No,' I whispered in response, 'um, no, not quite.'

I guess they do things differently in Pakistan; nevertheless, I was touched by her concern.

Late afternoon and I dropped by Sarah and Sara (whom I line-managed) for a final wrap-up of business. As I prepared to depart they produce a box of chocolates for me. I had no reason to think the chocolates were laced with a special paedo-poison and I accepted the gift graciously.

In my own office I packed up all my personal belongings (including my emergency jumper and spare shoes) to take away, fully aware that I might not return. As my solicitor colleague had said the previous day, if the case went to Crown Court it would take longer – two, three months, even six. At the back of my mind I wondered if the department would keep me on the books for such an extended period, let alone on full pay. I reduced my e-mail inbox to zero and cleared my computer of personal files. The only remaining file was a spreadsheet charting my annual leave – most of it used up with three weeks in China. It was bizarre to think I had treated my days of holiday leave like gold, now I was going to be absent for several months (even six?) on full pay.

Alone I walked down the stairs to the exit of the almost empty building. Once upon a time (in earlier administrative jobs) I had envisioned that there would be a day when I would walk down a corridor, descend a stairwell as a free man, finally removed from the work environment, never to work in administration again having secured (as far as one could) an ability to earn a living in the creative arts. It would be a triumphant, momentously momentous moment. But here I was, shuffling down the stairs in the fading light, shoulders stooped with a slight sense of nausea burning my insides perhaps never to return to a conventional working environment not because of progress or achievement, but because I was unemployable. With that, I exited the building and headed home to a life of 'special leave'.

At home, I threw my bag of personal belongings on the bed and slowly removed my tie. I normally slung it over the wardrobe door for use later in the week, but on this occasion I was aware I might not be leading a life which required a necktie, so I bundled it up along with others and buried them deep in the wardrobe. The only ties I would be wearing in the next six months would be in a court in a display of respect for a judge and the judicial process. Holy cow.

Year Three (Y3): August

Y3: August: 1. Special Leave

I was determined to be productive while also trying to enjoy my new-found 'freedom'. Turning over courtroom scenarios in my head as I paced about the house on Saturday morning, I soon realised the morning was slipping away and I walked into town for a coffee with my notebooks and iPad.

There was only really one place in town in which I could stand to sit (as it were), the King Alfred's Bar. Finding a bench-table-combo in the beer garden bathed in warm sunshine and with the weary sigh of a sailor signing up to twelve months at sea, I sat, opened my new notebook and started to write notes on the case. Thoughts had been blowing around my head like kites in the wind; I needed to tie them down, tether them to a plan. They needed to be organised not only for myself but also for any solicitor. The solicitor would know nothing about me, the case against me or my difficulties in Meadow Road. To a solicitor my case was just another job.

As recommended by both my eldest brother and my work colleague (and former solicitor) Michael, I had decided that a meeting with my own solicitor before the court appearance was something I certainly wanted to do. A meeting with my solicitor had been had therefore been arranged (scheduled for five days later – the day before my first appearance in the Magistrate's Court on Friday). There were a number of questions, issues, topics that I wanted to cover. So, warmed by a beer and sun, I started writing up notes beginning with the question 'Why was I being held responsible for the offence and not other computer users?' followed by an agenda for discussion, notes and lists including: a first list of 'questions and statements' for the defence; a 'to do' list for the solicitor; profiles of Anna T. Mannheim (the prime suspect in my opinion) and Ian Linklee; a summary of my video clips relating to Mannheim and Linklee at Meadow Road; a summary of all the available evidence supporting the defence; a summary of 'possible' evidence supporting the defence (i.e. leads to be investigated) and a list of what to look out for at the first court hearing.

By lunchtime I began to feel better but, although more productive on Sunday, by Sunday evening I started to note a creeping doubt and within an hour I was overwhelmed by every aspect of the case. All my deliberations became disconcerting.

Though bewildered and challenged by doubt, a part of me kept referring me back to my other instinctive, unequivocal response to the images shown to me by the police nine and a half months after my arrest. Michael Bull's words 'have faith in yourself' also came back to me, but it failed to alleviate my nervousness entirely. I wanted to have a clear conscience if and/or when I formally pointed the finger at Mannheim. Above all, I wanted to point to something showing that the police's thesis was inherently flawed.

The anxiety generated by the absence of information was compounded by the fact that I was conscious that I was becoming anxious. It was self-perpetuating. Furthermore, I was aware that to continue on such a journey (of four, five, six months) culminating in a public Crown Court trial was a seriously challenging prospect. I felt I could muddle through the stress, but that was not enough. I wanted to be confident. I wanted to be clear in the delivery of my defence.

Just as I was wallowing in this uncertainty and pondering my inner-strength, I found myself in my bedroom sorting through miscellaneous piles of papers in which I hoped there might be something of use for my defence. One pile of travel documents, dating to eighteen months before the police knocked on my door (a time of innocence), related to two weeks I had spent on a group tour in Morocco. One traveller in the group was a sweet, twenty-something Japanese girl, Emi. On the last night in Essanouia the tour group had sat around on the hotel's roof terrace eating and drinking. A local tattooist arrived to tattoo members of the group with mementoes of our time in the country. On a small scrap of paper Emi had translated my name into Japanese script for the henna tattoos for my upper arms. Translated, my name, 'David', meant 'The Big Dipper' which in turn, she had noted on the paper, translated as reliable and resourceful. It was a good, little timely reminder; I felt I could be both reliable and resourceful. So, with that little nod of encouragement I resolved to put together a compelling case for review by the solicitor four days later on Thursday.

Y3: August: 2. The 'August Document'

During that first week of August I extended the document of notes and questions to nine pages (with an agenda) which covered the following:

    i.   The question: What should I expect on my first appearance in the Magistrate's Court. (I wanted to be prepared and not look like a rabbit squaring up against an oncoming 4x4);

    ii.   A summary of the case as I saw it. This was a short explanation designed for an outsider about Mannheim and why, to my mind, she was perfectly capable of being behind it;

   iii. Questions and Statements (& Notes) for the Defence. This document would act as a checklist of questions or notes that might be relevant to the hearing. My solicitor would have other cases running that day, but my case was hopefully the one and only case I would face in my lifetime. It was particularly important because it would define the remaining decades of my life. I wanted the solicitor to be sceptical of everything the prosecution said in court;

iv. Summary of Evidence and Facts. A simple summary of the available hard evidence and other easily provable facts;

v. Summary of the evidence in the 'Mannheim Theory' including notes on the video clips and evidence of fraudulent activity;

vi. Post-court. A discussion item on the procedures and options after the court appearance;

vii. 'To do' list – Solicitor & Defendant. A list of things to be done either by myself or by the solicitor. I could conduct some investigation, but other investigations would have to be done through proper legal channels. In an ideal world, the solicitor would engage the services of a private investigator, but I was getting the sense that the world in which I had landed wasn't that kind of world;

viii. I also included appendices giving details on Anna Mannheim, the video clips (their content and context as part of the 'Mannheim Theory') and finally a list of the dates that I had been required to answer bail at the police station (a total of fourteen, including the day on which I was not re-bailed, but charged).

With the solicitor charging £200 per hour (plus VAT at 20%) I wanted to make my minutes count, I thought an agenda would focus the discussion. Hopefully the very act of compiling this documentation would demonstrate that I was serious about my predicament and defence. It would also give the solicitor a clear idea of where I was coming from and what to look for in any dossier made available by the Crown Prosecution Service (CPS).

My documentation started with a summary of my legal situation, followed by my living arrangements in the previous ten years and then a summary of the main facts, including: there was one computer on which there were 'deleted/inaccessible' images; the computer had been in a shared house with no internal lockable doors and that the alleged offender (i.e. me) had had serious difficulty with housemates at the time. The difficulties had been well documented by the defendant who possessed supporting evidence comprised of emails, letters and video footage which, it was hoped, would be complemented by information forthcoming from the City Council, the landlord and even the police themselves. I explained that the 'intelligence' that had led to my arrest had not been shared (nearly 2 years and 6 months from arrest) even though it had been specifically requested twice by me on that first day.

I included the one-page summary statement that I had sent to duty solicitor Alex Watt eleven months after my arrest in which I had stated the images and screen grabs shown to me during the second police interview had been new to me. Trying to be objective, I listed the possible explanations for the images on my computer: 'The defendant was crazy' (i.e. in denial), but I firmly discounted this argument. (I only included it to demonstrate my objectivity and tackle the issue head on); a computer virus; computer use by visitors to the house; identity theft (credit card) or other, or lastly, the 'Mannheim Theory', my firm favourite and, to my mind, the only credible theory.

I started the next section (entitled 'Statements, Questions and Notes for the Defence) by asking the question: 'why am I here?' after which I summarised the relevant points, asking questions where necessary.

i. Computer: There was nothing 'live' on the computer or on the other computer seized, a MacBook Pro laptop. Nothing had been found on 200 plus DVDs, numerous CDs, memory sticks, 300 gigabyte external hard-drives. The only device that had the deleted and inaccessible images had not been password-protected, had no-encryption and was based in a shared house.

ii. Intelligence: What had been the 'intelligence' that had triggered the police investigation in the first place? (I had a problem using the word 'intelligence' preferring 'information' or other. The word 'intelligence' implied a credibility – something clever, authoritative and therefore accurate.) Had the 'information' come from a website? Was it a record of a credit card transaction? Or had it been a tip-off (anonymous or otherwise)?

iii. Computer users: What investigation has been undertaken on the other computer users? Was the 'intelligence' (or 'information') specific to me (the person) or had it been specific to the computer (or even the property address)?

iv. Time: Why had it taken two years and five months to investigate and charge? Did that suggest a weak case? Or that my case was not a priority? The police had been unable to 'pin down' what had happened, said DC Woods to my parents during a visit to Shrub Lane two years into the investigation. I explained in the document that the delay made it difficult to pull together evidence and witnesses dating back 5 years earlier. In that time I had changed jobs twice, moved house and changed storage arrangements three times. Furthermore, former colleagues who might have been able to assist me in recalling my movements had also moved on and, no doubt, been preoccupied with events in their own lives. Not to mention, people's memories fail.

While I had been away in China a British High Court Ruling (June 2011) had stated that arrested persons must be charged within 96 hours (four days) of arrest if at all. In other words the maximum time a person could remain on police bail was four days. For me it had been two years, five months and two weeks. The day on which I was scheduled to appear in court for the first time would have been a cool 899 days since my arrest. When I received a dossier from the Crown Prosecution Service on their case against me, the police (with unlimited resources relative to my own) would still have had a 900 day head-start on me. Furthermore, the 'preliminary file' of evidence (as described by DC Woods two weeks earlier) was not the whole story. Information was yet to be disclosed, in other words, it was currently 'withheld'. Surely, any further delay to this matter was not appropriate, I exclaimed (on paper).

In the document, I dared to describe myself as 'of good character' and made a plea for a sympathetic ear: I had had no previous arrests or interaction with police (possibly in contrast to the other computer users). I explained that I had lost two and a half years of my life, completely lost momentum of my life's work (the film screened at London's bfi Southbank) and, needless to say, endured the stress of the case while obediently making myself available for thirteen scheduled interviews of which twelve had been cancelled by the police.

Y3: August: 3. The 'August Document' (Cont.)

The next section of the 'August document' summarised the 'Evidence and Facts' of the case as I understood them. For emphasis, I purposefully repeated some observations already listed in the previous section hoping it allowed the lists to work independently of each other.

Computer: Although largely a repeat of the previous section, I also noted that there had been no social networking activity on the computer. I referred to the possible existence of some pictures of (clothed) women. It had started with an Internet search for the 'Pearl and Dean' Malibu drinks commercial constantly played in 1980s cinemas. I had managed to save a few screen-grabs of my benchmark beauty 'Auntie Beryl' who had haunted me since my teens. More recently Auntie Beryl had been joined by others including a dinner guest in a Jaguar car commercial; actress Jennifer Beals (of the movie *Flashdance*) and others. I was also careful to note that the average age of the women was approximately 30 years old (with, in fact, Jennifer Beals being older than me).

I described how dozens of people had had interaction with the seized computer over the years, including Anna T. Mannheim. I referred to the shared house with no lockable interior doors. I explained that on the day of arrest the search warrant covered the whole house and outbuildings, yet the police searched only one room, my car and partially searched the office. There had been no searching of the attic, garage, shed, other rooms and no searching of the lockup-storage unit over the road mentioned to the police during their search and questioning. At the beginning of the visit the arresting officer explained that all the computer equipment would be taken, but after approximately forty-five minutes in my company, she had decided the officers would take two computers and *leave* two computers.

I described how in the police station just before the interview on the day of arrest the 'Arrest/Charge sheet' (or whatever it was called) had been blank except for one phrase taken out of context. The phrase had been printed in

UPPERCASE presumably to lend it significance (suggesting the words amounted to an 'admission' rather than the speculative guess). It had been a wholly throwaway comment (among several) about why the police might have turned up at my door. The words were:

'I MIGHT HAVE HAD POP-UPS AND MAYBE I CLICKED SOMETHING.'

There was no reference to the delivery of the words, their intonation, their context nor to my vocalised bewilderment at the police visit and statement that I had not come across such 'stuff' on the Internet. I recounted that in the interview none of the questions asked of me indicated the police had any information whatsoever other than my name, the allegation, the year of the alleged offence and the location (Meadow Road). It was a 'fishing expedition' in the words of solicitor, Alison Walcott, at the time.

I then described DC Chris Woods' behaviour on the day of the second interview, nine months after arrest. When I was being 'booked in' for interview (and my person and belongings searched) the custody officer had found two memory sticks that I had been carrying. He had immediately asked DC Woods whether the memory sticks should be confiscated, but DC Woods had casually shaken his head declining the offer, all of which I had taken as a good sign. I had speculated that perhaps the interview was a formality before matters were to be wrapped up.

I then presented a summary of the (possible) useable evidence (of varying degrees of verifiability) supporting the Mannheim Theory.

A 'Known Known': Anna T. Mannheim was a known user of the computer in Meadow Road. I had allowed her to use the computer, albeit with reluctance. A 'Known Unknown':

Mannheim's use of the computer in my absence was not known. There were examples of harassment, threats and aggression shown to myself, her boyfriend (Ian Linklee) and (by telephone) towards a Kent-based/Dover-based garage that had been repairing her vehicle and evidence of benefit fraud (which was thwarted by me, the defendant).

I listed other evidence that might have been forthcoming after some investigation, including the appearance of pop-up dialogue boxes on the seized computer warning that someone was trying to gain control of the computer. I speculated about the existence of County Court Judgments (or similar) submitted *by* Mannheim against others. (It might suggest a pattern of a behaviour, after all, it was her boyfriend, Ian Linklee, who had said 'This is what she does' when I queried her aggressive phone call to the garage.) Similarly, County Court Judgments submitted *against* Mannheim might also be helpful. I was aware that two Credit Agencies and Linklee's mobile phone company had been chasing them after their departure. Who knew what evidence was lurking 'out there' waiting to be scooped up in my legal defence.

The 'To Do' list (for both the Solicitor and myself) contained duplications to empathise certain points while simultaneously allowing the list to work independently of others. The list included the acquisition of:

i.   video and audio recordings of the defendant (me) in the police station during the Mannheim tenancy seeking advice on my Meadow Road difficulties;

ii. the recordings of the two telephone calls between the defendant and the police the same month regarding the Meadow Road difficulties;

iii. any remaining evidence from the police (which might have useful information, tips, details/facts to be challenged, or avenues to be explored);

   iv. documents from the City Council (including correspondence between the defendant and the City Council) relating to the Mannheim benefit fraud;

   v.   copies of any interaction between the defendant and the Meadow Road landlord regarding the difficulties in the property (including discussions around the installation of locks on internal and external doors);

   vi. Finally, I referred to the two occasions the defendant had witnessed the on-screen pop-ups warning that 'someone is trying to gain control of the computer'.

I listed the materials that were already available for review by the solicitor, including: my contemporaneous video diaries of the Meadow Road difficulties; some email correspondence between myself and the landlord, and myself and the City Council regarding the difficulties and benefit fraud. I listed separately the materials that might be available for review by the solicitor in due course, many of which would require investigation beforehand either by the defendant or the solicitor (such as testimony from the Dover-based garage mechanic regarding Mannheim's abusive phone calls).

The appendices included a profile of Anna T. Mannheim (the most vicious, unpleasant, scheming person I had ever met) and the history of the living arrangements for Meadow Road including the deterioration of the relationship between myself and the co-tenants (rent was not being paid and my requests to discuss the matter were being ignored) hence the approach to police for guidance.

I worked hard at preparing the materials (agenda papers, DVDs of video clips) during Monday and Tuesday. As I edited together the video clips I felt miserable. Apple's Final Cut Pro editing software had been purchased to edit the two feature-length movies shot in the 2000s. The movies themselves were now languishing on computer drives in a police evidence lock-up; I felt that the editing of these clips for a criminal court was a debasement of the precious software technology and its potential.

On Wednesday I finalised the documents and drove the following day to the offices of my solicitor 24 hours ahead of my first court appearance at the Magistrate's Court (which, if I haven't mentioned it already, was 899 days after my arrest).

Y3: August: 4. Solicitor Warren Meeting

Having parked in a multi-story car-park near the town centre I got lost in the small streets of Abingdon and so popped into a newsagents to ask the whereabouts of Stratford Street.

'Stratford Street?' the shop assistant thought (but in my own head), 'that's where the criminal law solicitors are based, isn't it?'

The words (which never left her mouth) echoed around the insides of my skull then plummeted south, ripping through any organ on the way, arriving with a thump in my stomach.

The shop assistant told me to head up the street, turn left and keep left where I would see Stratford Street right opposite the pub.

She thought (again, in my head) that she had artfully disguised what she had been thinking – that the man standing opposite her asking for directions was most probably guilty of the crime of which he had been accused. But she didn't care what crime (as long as it didn't involve children).

I jogged up the street, took the turns, found the street and the Blacker McCann offices. It was exactly 10.00 a.m.. I had hoped to get there ten minutes early, to show I was keen and ready to get started, but I had failed. A brass plaque was attached to the wall by the door to the offices – Blacker McCann Criminal Law. Although the street was empty I looked this way and that before furtively entering the premises, itself snuggled into an unbroken terraced street of old town-centre buildings. It is not something anyone wants to be seen doing – entering the offices of criminal law specialists. I introduced myself to the two receptionists while wondering how long they had known about me. No doubt my name had been bandied around the offices for a few years.

A request to visit the gents meant that I was shown upstairs and found myself negotiating my way up and down little staircases and passageways catching sight of staff tucked away in small spaces. Although 'cottage-y-cosiness' is a nice environment for a charity or a small design business, I did wonder where all the money was supposed to be. They were supposed to be criminal lawyers, right? Weren't they supposed to be in shiny, glass-fronted buildings which showed-off their successful track record in a brash vulgar fashion? I was pricked by worry. I didn't want to get my choice of defence team wrong. Returning to the reception area, I sat and waited pondering my solicitor's credentials until one of the senior partners, Warren Blacker, arrived, apologised for the delay and escorted me into a small meeting room which appeared to doubled as the firm's computer server room.

'Sorry for the noisy room,' he said, 'we are soon to move offices.'

Okay, I nodded and smiled as I inwardly relaxed. I hoped the brass plaque in the new offices shouted, 'f*ck-off criminal lawyers, look at my new shiny building,' to passers-by.

Warren was a tall, slim man in his late-fifties, with a slight Australian accent, but he soon dropped into the conversation that he had been practising law in the UK for 25-plus years which was a relief. The company bore his name so it couldn't have been so bad. Gentle and calm in manner, he had a slight stoop owing possibly to a predisposition to leaning forward when listening to his clients.

I pulled out my papers explaining that I had prepared an agenda. I was fully aware that it might appear officious, but I was paying for the privilege of sixty minutes of his time and I just wanted to crack on.

I had no intention of dwelling on the items listed in the nine-page document. He could read it later if he so wished, but I hoped my work demonstrated to him that I was organised, proactive and taking my predicament seriously.

'I realise that a lot of this is irrelevant for tomorrow,' I sighed, referring to my first appearance in the Magistrate's Court, 'but I want to put all this information on your radar. It might help when reviewing any dossier from the Crown Prosecution Service. Something might pop out.'

(I was in fact thinking of something related to Mannheim and/or the 'intelligence'.)

'I also want you to know what is going on in my head.'

We began with item one on the agenda 'Procedures', i.e. what would happen at the first court hearing (the following day).

'There are a few things which will happen tomorrow,' Warren explained. 'The first being we could enter a plea. Secondly, the jurisdiction will be determined i.e. whether the case will be heard in a Magistrate's Court or the Crown Court. After the hearing there will be an adjournment for approximately six weeks after which you shall appear again at the Magistrate's Court for a short administrative meeting whereupon it will be passed up to the Crown Court. At that second hearing in the Magistrate's Court the Crown Prosecution Service (CPS) will produce 'committal papers' outlining the prosecution's case with a view to moving the case up the Crown Court. Four weeks after that there will be a first appearance at a Crown Court where a date for the trial will be set.'

I winced at the reference to a trial. It still felt bizarre, surreal.

I ran through the remaining items at a pace waiting for Warren to stop me if there anything piqued his interest. I was conscious of the cost of his time and besides, as Warren had said, nothing could be done at this stage. I still had his colleague's (Alex Watt's) words echoing in my ears – 'we are all reactive'.

At the bottom of page one I listed the three theories addressing the presence of the deleted images on the computer: The defendant was crazy (but, I pointed out to Warren, I did not accept this; I was only trying to be reasonable and open-minded. Listing me first would do that, I hoped.) Secondly: an 'unknown' – a virus; visitors to the house; identity theft (credit card), other. And, finally, the 'Mannheim Theory'.

I explained that I had been vexed, confused, bewildered when I walked into the police interview room (for the second interview), but, having been shown a sample of 22 recovered images, it became crystal clear that it was all completely new to me. I recounted walking out of that interview room calm, collected and with a clear conscience, in fact, even relieved that I finally knew the truth. (Or felt I knew the truth – Mannheim.)

I explained that I did not want to point the finger at anyone, but if and/or when I did, I wanted to do so with a clear conscience. This was the phrasing I had come up with in the previous 48 hours while pacing about the house. This particular phrase I attributed to the bathroom. Other defence strategies and phrases were born in different parts of the house. Every corner of the house could lay claim to contributing to the defence strategy. Who needs moorland, windy beaches and mountain ranges for inspiration when you have a bedroom, bathroom, living room, kitchen and even a landing. Nevertheless, I did feel it was important to establish phrases that accurately reflected my position. So, yes, if and/or when I pointed the finger I wanted to do so with a clear conscience. In the meantime, I was prepared to absorb the heat, I told Warren.

He was looking at me. I had been getting used to this searching look for truth or guilt. I knew there would be more of it in due course from all quarters. There would come a point in the not-too-distant future (minutes away possibly) that he would be reaching a judgement on my innocence or guilt. Alex had done the same only twenty months before. I guessed that Warren had sat across the table from a great many people over the years and come to many judgments about their characters. I couldn't say I liked it, but being judged came with the territory (a criminal charge) and was something to be endured. I was not sure how I came across, I didn't really care, but I stayed firm and met his gaze. That said, it was a tireless battle.

Warren didn't ask about the video clips, but when I showed him the bail dates noting that the following day would be 899 days since of my arrest (having been re-bailed thirteen times), he muttered 'Awful,' shaking his head.

Warren explained that the computer would be sent to their own experts to determine how the images had arrived on the computer and any context. However, these computer experts would be engaged later during the Crown Court stage when I would be eligible for Legal Aid. It was not advisable to spend money ahead of time. I noted his guidance, but it unnerved me a little. I would have rather cracked on and had the experts involved as soon as possible. Alison Walcott (the solicitor I met on the day of my arrest) would be looking after my case.

'Counsel is engaged later at the Crown Court stage.'

I must have look worried, because Warren again advised me that there was no point spending money engaging Counsel ahead of getting Legal Aid (when my case was 'committed' to Crown Court).

'So,' I asked, quietly, 'will it go to trial before December?'

'Let's see,' said Warren, doing the sums. 'Six weeks after the first hearing tomorrow will be mid-September for the second hearing in Magistrate's Court; that means a Crown Court appearance in mid-October to enter a plea. At that Crown Court hearing the judge will set a time-scale for the trial, so no, I don't think it will be this year.'

Wow. Five months away at least.

'When you first appear at the Crown Court you will enter a plea. You will be informed that the plea you enter will have an impact on the possible sentence. It will be reduced if you plead guilty on that date (by up to a third) and diminish further and further up to the beginning of the trial.'

Pleading guilty wasn't going to happen at any stage and I 'sort of' knew I wouldn't bottle it either.

'Anything else for tomorrow?' I asked

'No, we'll see what the prosecution pack shows. But this,' said Warren tapping my nine-page August document, 'is a useful starting point.'

I suspected he was trying to be nice by not dismissing all the work that I had put in, but I detected that he felt that computer forensics was the key. Although an understandable position for a legal professional, I nevertheless hoped that he would also take my position (i.e. preferred theory) seriously. That said, Warren did refer to how programmes and materials could be downloaded to the ignorance of the user. 'Trojans' could subsequently gain control of a computer.

'We have a Trojan case going on at the moment,' he said nonchalantly.

Intrigued (and aghast), I explained that I had wondered whether my credit card details had been stolen and used to purchase material.

'Credit cards do not have to be used to buy anything,' said Warren, 'merely used to register on sites.'

I sat and listened to (and paid for) Warren as he related more stories including fights between defence forensics and the police; in one recent case the police forensics lab would not release the computer to the defence team for review at all. The police had said the defence expert must visit the police lab to examine the machine.

''No way' was the defence response,' said Warren. 'There have been some real tussles.'

F*ck.

'Then there was the report by our own computer experts that was not accepted by the prosecution.'

Really? Holy cow.

'In another case we submitted a forensics report to the Crown Prosecution Service (CPS) eight weeks ago but we still haven't had a response yet. We go to trial in ten days.'

This was something I hadn't really considered. Why would the police, the Crown Prosecution drag their feet in such a way? Wouldn't they embrace all challenges to their own findings? To ensure that justice was served? It left me feeling confused and defeatist, in part because I knew that the legal to-ing and fro-ing was beyond my control and all of it taking up precious time and taxpayers' money. Fears began to bubble up in me that the judicial process was separate, distinct from the common man's understanding of 'justice'.

Y3: August: 5. Solicitor Warren Meeting (Cont.)

'There are a number of things I want from the court hearing tomorrow,' I said. 'Firstly, why do the police think it is me (and not the others in the house)? Secondly, what was the 'intelligence' that triggered the police visit?'

'No,' replied Warren. 'After reviewing the prosecution papers we can plan.'

'Do I get a copy of the papers?'

'Yes, we send everything to you.'

'When you were arrested, did they say it was part of an investigation?' he asked. 'Operation Ore, or something?'

'No,' I replied.

Was that a good sign, I wondered? If it had been part of an operation, then the police might have referred to it, but they hadn't, which suggested my case was a standalone investigation? I found that I was doing a lot of thinking privately during the meeting with Warren. I didn't want to say much, rather absorb information while not giving the impression of total ignorance. I was still very much acclimatising to my new-found legal status and predicament.

'There is not much to do tomorrow,' Warren explained, snapping me out of my musings. 'The police probably won't be there. It will be some drone who wouldn't know much about the case. At the second meeting in six weeks, the CPS makes a prima facie case for trial and submit the 'committal papers'.'

'Why doesn't it go straight to Crown Court after tomorrow?' I asked.

'Good question; it's historical. In the past the CPS would bring witnesses to court so the Magistrate could assess the competence and strength of the case, but that practice has been discontinued partly due to cost. The procedures have not caught up yet. Also, the CPS would not want to potentially demonstrate the weaknesses in a case.'

But wasn't that the point? Once again, I found myself thinking the weaknesses should be out in the open, allowing them to be addressed, challenged and debated all in the name (and pursuit) of justice?

I didn't bother sharing my thoughts with Warren. I was getting the idea of this brave new world.

Having listened to Warren for nearly an hour and sensing he was not focussing on my preferred theory, I steered the subject of the conversation to the phone calls I had made to the police during the Linklee-Mannheim tenancy. My reasons for contacting the police had been two-fold, I explained to Warren: firstly, to seek advice and, secondly, to put the matter on the police's 'radar'. It had been clear to me that the relationship would continue to deteriorate and I feared for 'my situation'.

'It is not make or break,' said Warren, unimpressed. 'It is the equivalent of hearsay.'

I don't fight my corner, in part, because I don't want to come across as desperate (just yet).

'It doesn't prove anything,' he continued matter-of-factly. Too matter-of-factly for my liking.

It still put me out, but I remained quiet. How could it not prove anything (I didn't say)? At the very least it proved I had had concerns that were communicated to the police two years before my arrest and in the time-period of the alleged offence (I continued not to say). His take on such a crucial bit of evidence (which had sustained me for years) rankled, but I grudgingly understood where he was coming from.

'Did they issue a crime number?' he asked.

'No, I don't think so,' I said, before sharing further details.

I had spoken to a sympathetic woman who had given me advice during the two calls. I had asked for (and had written down) a code/reference number at the time. The officer had given something like 'PC1234 White' over the phone. (Or, at least, I believed the reference number wording had had something do with 'white' or a colour). At the time I assumed the colour was a code related to a category of phone call. Having asked for a reference number, I had assumed that was what I had been given, but when I had phoned back a day or so later and gave the 'reference number', the police officer had said 'yes, that's me'. So perhaps it was the officer's name.

I explained to Warren that we might be able to trace my calls (in the police records) using my mobile phone number or track down a 'PC White' (in case 'white' did identify a person after all). We might be able to get the female police officer to testify to my troubles and even play the recordings of the calls in court, I explained. Warren didn't seem remotely interested, saying he would be very surprised if the calls had indeed been recorded.

I let it go.

As we worked through my papers I noted that Warren only marked one paragraph – the one regarding the appearance of pop-up dialogue boxes warning me that someone was trying to gain control to the computer. It was ironic. I had not mentioned the pop-ups to anyone else other than the solicitor, nor had I intended to, because I had no way of proving their appearance to anyone. Every other defence argument in the document in front of him was supported by a video clip, a document or an email. The one bullet point he chose to mark, I was unable to support with independent evidence.

Towards the end of the meeting Warren raised the matter of money and repeated pretty much what Raquel had said to me over the telephone. I didn't qualify for any Legal Aid as I progressed through the Magistrate's Courts, but I would qualify at the Crown Court stage. In the past Legal Aid had not been not means-tested, but now it was. Warren took details of my salary as I explained that my work (and salary) circumstances might change. Until that time I would be required to make a contribution to the legal costs (of the State prosecuting me).

'Do you have a partner?' Warren asked.

'No,' I replied.

'Single?'

I nodded. Yes.

'Do you have someone who you can talk to?'

'I have family, but I don't want to talk too much to them.'

'It can help. It will get very stressful as things go on. Have you seen a doctor? You ought to.'

'I think I'll be okay. I've survived two and a half years so far,' I muttered. 'I tend to compartmentalise.'

'You're lucky.'

Um, I feel it.

The meeting over, we rose to our feet. As we left the room I asked Warren what I could do in the coming weeks. Should I prepare more documentation for him?

'You can write as much as you want. Comment on any aspect of the CPS dossier.'

Good, but that was still daunting. Would the CPS documents be all legal gobbledegook or technical terms? Warren seemed to think everything would be based around the computer. Which was good. And crap. Of course I wanted him to test the technical side of the prosecution's case (ideally unearthing anything that would kill the prosecution's case), but what if the technical stuff was ambiguous? A matter of interpretation? Indifferent? I also needed Warren and the defence team to take the Mannheim Theory seriously. As gospel. The woman must have figured in all this, but right then it counted for nothing.

Even though I had a clearer view of the situation, I had no peace of mind. I was conscious of the upcoming developments – court hearings, CPS papers. Was I going to be spooked?

Unnerved? There might have been nothing (or even worse, absolutely nothing) that indicated Mannheim's involvement, but I also knew that the police were selective when presenting information and 'evidence'. So, I needed to brace myself to be spooked, unsettled.

Warren explained that he would be a bit late getting to the court, but his colleague would be there.

'We'll try and get you out as soon as possible. It is not a nice place to hang around.'

Really? I thought of drunks and low-lifes, even 'paedos', who were making court appearances, no doubt all protesting their innocence.

It was bizarre to think that at that time the following day, 11.30 a.m., I would know where I stood. And then? What would happen over the following five months? Very possibly the events would give an indication of how I would live the next fifty years. The events in court might have been the most important moment in the whole shebang and be more influential on my state-of-mind than any police interview.

'So, yes, write anything,' said Warren. 'It all goes to the barrister.'

We part ways for 240 quid (including VAT – the Government's charge to me for the privilege of paying for legal guidance on how to defend myself against an allegation about which I know nothing and they know 'everything'.) [sigh].

In the reception we bumped into his colleague, Kristen, who would be at the Magistrate's Court the following day. She was happy and smiley and polite. No judgment there. Or at least it wasn't apparent. Professional, I suppose, as were the staff at the coffee shop around the corner five minutes later. That said, it could all be different the following day when my predicament reached the public domain. I speculated that the coffee I ordered might be the last I would have as a private citizen, a respectable customer. My next coffee might be purchased by a 'notorious abuser' (that was assuming I was able to find anyone who would serve me coffee).

Y3: August: 6. Magistrate's Court

Twenty-two hours later I walked into the Magistrate's Court around the corner from the police station and Crown Court. I passed through a metal detector to be frisked by a guard. Having climbed the stairs to the first floor I arrived in a small hall area off which, on one side, were a few courtrooms accessed through double doors. On the other side of the hall numerous doors led to consulting room and offices. The hall area itself was more like a dowdy waiting area in a bus station or a sports centre in a slummy side of town. Having introduced myself to the reception desk, I was told to take a seat at the end of the hall on one of the rows of double-backed benches outside the courtroom assigned for my hearing.

During the twenty-minute wait before my hearing I counted nearly thirty people in attendance (alleged offenders and families), but I was the only person wearing a suit and tie. After a few minutes, my solicitor, Kristen, found me and we slipped into a consultation room. After she had given me a brief outline of the upcoming hearing I asked to review the papers that had been passed to her by the Crown Prosecution Service (CPS).

Kristen handed the papers over and I skimmed through their contents. I was looking for two things: information relating to the 'intelligence' that had triggered the whole investigation and, secondly, a witness statement from Linklee and/or Mannheim. The police had certainly known about Ian and his live-in girlfriend from comments made in the kitchen on the day of my arrest to DC Hopkins and the comments made to

DC Woods when he had visited my parents to question my father two years later. If the police had seen fit to interview my father as a possible computer-user then Linklee and Mannheim would certainly have been interviewed, but would the police release the statements?

The CPS papers included the general bail notices, the criminal charge notice, a handwritten witness statement signed by my father, the interview notes by the arresting officer, DC Lauren Hopkins (which looked broadly accurate but, as expected, it mentioned the 'I might have had pop-ups ...' sentence) and a short computer report which described how the computer was interrogated, details of the downloaded images noting that their date-stamps were not available. It referred to some websites that were 'suggestive of content' and access to my email accounts which was unsettling, but not surprising (I had never denied the computer was mine). But on this first skim, there was nothing about the 'intelligence' and no statements from the co-tenants Linklee and Mannheim.

Kristen recommended that we entered a 'no plea' at the hearing which left me feeling conflicted. Wasn't that perceived as weak? Didn't I want to take the fight to them?

'You can enter a 'not guilty' plea if you wish,' Kristen said, 'but by entering a 'no plea' now we can see what else the CPS has in the other papers which will follow at the next hearing in six weeks time.'

I paused and thought. Did I follow my general rule that I heed the advice of experts? I was of an age where I followed the advice of doctors, car mechanics, builders and technicians just as I encouraged others to heed my advice on matters on which I was relatively expert. Legal advice was no different, I supposed; might as well add 'criminal lawyers' to the list.

Okay, I said, yes, I was happy to follow the advice, but I did not feel terribly comfortable. I understood that it was 'advisable' to keep options open, but I knew that keeping options open was more for the benefit of the solicitors. I suspected that they were not convinced of my line of defence but it did not worry me greatly. I welcomed scepticism. I didn't want a solicitor who didn't have a healthy scepticism about all matters (while simultaneously being robust and professional in my defence). Nevertheless, I was beginning to feel more like a passenger in the whole thing. Let them do their job.

I returned to the waiting area still feeling over-dressed and waited for my call. The majority of those waiting for hearings appeared to be Eastern European or Russian: there was a man limping, another with his arm in a sling, another seemingly drunk, another with numerous teeth missing, but perhaps I was being unkind. Other than the 'advocates' (legal representatives), there was only one other man in a suit (albeit with cheap shoes). This gave me some comfort until I heard him talk in an Eastern European accent.

As I waited I reflected on upcoming events. I would not have any leads to pursue from the papers passed to me by Kristen: no 'intelligence', no other witness statements. The papers had contained the very barest of information.

Then crystal clear over the tannoy: 'David Anderson to Court One, please.'

I rose from my seat and strode purposefully towards the courtroom door thinking, f*ck, did everyone hear that? F*ck. At least they hadn't read out the charge, but checked myself just in case my gratitude was premature. I walked through the double doors following Kristen into the courtroom itself. I slowed waiting to be shown where to stand. Kristen pointed up a few steps into what looked like a glass-box with folding benches.

'You go into the dock,' she said not quite aware of the effect such an instruction had on me.

The courtroom was like all the courtrooms on television. Purpose-built, large with décor dating to the 1970s when criminals were criminals. Three Magistrates sat on the raised bench on the far side of the room.

A shop window it wasn't, but it might as well have been. I was now on display to the world.

So, here I was, 899 days after my arrest and my troubles were now in the public domain. It could be in the local newspapers within hours. I was slap-bang in the middle of a life-defining event. The State was squared up across the table against little ol' me, and, owing to the nature of the charge, it felt as if they had little to do to ensure a 'result' and my life as I knew it (and had planned it) would be over. And all, as far as I was concerned, *all* because of the benefits cheat, Anna T. Mannheim.

Anyway, it was game on. I had to pull all my wits about me to prepare my case and blow the suckers to kingdom come.

END

Continued in …

MAD

AS

HELL

Part Two: 215 Days

ACKNOWLEDGEMENTS

In addition to thanking friends and family for their support during the troubles (or 'Pickle'), thanks are also due to a handful of people who have reviewed or assisted in the production of these books. They include Dr R.R. for reviewing a draft of Part One and recommending structural and stylistic changes and Grace Fussell http://gracefusselldesign.com/ for the book cover(s). Others deserving a nod for miscellaneous support are JAG, PJB and DMAG.

About the Author

For information on the author and other titles, please see:

http://www.madashell.website/

Facebook: http://tinyurl.com/z5er8wj
Twitter: https://twitter.com/MadAsHellBook

Lightning Source UK Ltd.
Milton Keynes UK
UKOW01f2343160817
307459UK00001B/34/P